Catholic Dad

For my parents, who taught me these lessons,
For my kids, who make them matter.

"Love begins by taking care of the closest ones—the ones at home."

Mother Teresa

Introduction

The stories in this book are tales of faith and family—which also means humor. Within the sacred circle of the family are experienced some of life's deepest and most profound moments, and also some of life's highest pinnacles of hilarity. Whether sublime or silly (and sometimes both at once), one thing is certain: this baffling, puzzling, sometimes exasperating, sometimes illuminating, and always interesting experience of fatherhood is a joyous adventure, a sacred trust, a divine mystery, and an amazing blessing.

These stories are drawn from several generations and several families, including my grandparents, parents, my own childhood, my kids, and tales from siblings, friends, and extended family. In my retelling of these stories I've streamlined, omitted, and rearranged events, and otherwise taken literary license with various details, all for purposes of narrative, humor, and privacy—and especially to draw out the comical inherent in the sometimes ridiculous situations of daily life (even if the humor can only be appreciated after the fact—and sometimes only long after the fact!).

I wrote these stories over a number of years, some reaching back more than a decade in first draft form. Others were completed just a few months before publication. I've arranged the stories thematically to roughly follow along with the calendar year and the feasts of the Church, rather than chronologically as the stories were written or the events transpired. Which means that you're seeing little snapshots of family life taken at different points in time over a long stretch of years, so in one story you might read about the antics of a pack of kids all running riot together, followed a few pages later by a story of our firstborn when fatherhood was all new. My family has also moved around quite a bit, and lived in different cities and different types of housing: townhouses, apartments, and several different single-family homes. So again, you'll see different domestic situations in different stories: one might describe life in a third floor apartment (with no elevator!), while another has us playing out in the backyard. It's all one family, just viewed at different points in its ever evolving lifecycle.

There are 52 stories in all, one for each week of the year, with those about particular holidays and feast days noted in the Table of Contents so you can find them easily. All the stories are freestanding, so you don't need to have read a previous story to follow the next. That way you can dip into the book when the inclination strikes and find something relevant to the season at hand, or follow along with one story a week throughout the year, or read the whole thing at one go, whatever works best for you.

I should also add a final note on memory—in particular, the reliability of my own, which has been hotly contested by family and friends after they've read these stories. To those (many) among my kith and kin who took issue with my recollection of events, I responded: write your own book!

I hope they don't.

Or maybe I hope they do, so I can see these same events through their eyes. Anyway, flawed or partial as my recollections may be, here they are, along with whatever lessons on fatherhood and family I've been able to glean from them. I hope you enjoy the journey!

I'd like to thank my Mom and Dad for helping edit and write many of these stories, and for sharing their ideas and suggestions, and most of all for sharing their wisdom—some of which even sunk in and made its way into these pages, though they've taught me more by their example than any dozens of books could ever contain or convey. I'd also like to thank my sisters for their editing help, and all my siblings for their encouragement and support.

Thank you also to the editors and writers who have helped me over the years, supported my work, taught me much, improved my writing, and given me a hand along the way, including: Danielle Bean, Kevin Cullen, Mary Kochan, Corrado Roeper, Patti McGuire Armstrong, Chelsea Zimmerman, David Paul Deavel, and many others too numerous to mention.

And of course, I'd like to thank my wife and kids.

"The family is placed at the center of the great struggle between good and evil, between life and death, between love and all that is opposed to love."

Blessed Pope John Paul II

1.

New Year's Day

Dream Big

One February I was at Waimea Bay on Oahu. There were monstrous waves. Truly gia-normous. I can tell you they were over 20 feet high, but you really have to see them yourself to understand. It's awe inspiring. Even I, fresh off the plane from a Midwest winter, my skin shining pale as an incandescent bulb, could feel it. There was a charge in the air, a wildness in the roar of the waves—a palpable sense of the ocean's majesty, its power.

Then, as I sat mesmerized, watching giant swells rise and curl over in a cascade of white, I saw something even more amazing: people. Out there. In the midst of that raging ocean.

My jaw dropped. Out there amid the towering waves, little specs of humanity bobbed up and down. And as I looked, I saw that they weren't just bobbing, they were surfing! They were actually riding those monster waves! I watched in eye-popping disbelief as surfers paddled furiously to *catch* those waves.

Occasionally some bedraggled surfer would stagger out of the water clutching half a broken board—only to grab a new board and head back out.

I was dumbfounded.

Who were these people?

Who sees an ocean heaving with 20 foot waves and thinks, "Hey, let's grab a stick of wood and jump in!"

But that's the way people are. They dream big. If you're born a surfer, you'll want to test yourself when the big breakers are pounding.

I was reminded of Waimea Bay when our first daughter was learning to crawl. And not just for the wipe-outs. It was her persistence, her effort, that made me think of the surfers. As many times as she fell, she got up to try again.

It made me think about what we fathers wish for our children. An easy way? With no risk, no worry? Or zest, daring, a lion's heart ready for big challenges? The kind of challenges that will demand from our children their very best, all they have, and all that they are—and then to see in our children the strength of character and fire in the belly that's eager to take on those challenges.

A real life, well lived, felt to the marrow.

Big dreams and the energy and courage to chase them.

Then if that's what we wish for our kids, what do we wish for ourselves? Mostly to win the lottery. Just kidding. (Sort of.) But really, going through our days sometimes we do more dreading than dreaming. Our thoughts can be more of avoiding— avoiding problems, avoiding fears, avoiding failure—than of working positively toward something good, let alone allowing thoughts of greatness touch our souls.

That's no way to chase big dreams.

And we've got big dreams to chase. Occasionally we lose sight of them, amid the thousand-and-one distractions clamoring for our attention. But we know they're there, even if we have to dig down to find them again.

Take the time to find them—and then get about the business of pursuing them.

When you do, know that it's not just for yourself. If you want your kids to be big dream chasers, show them how. They'll learn from watching you. If we want our kids to live with a lion's heart, we need to live that way ourselves.

And when you're working on your dreams, remember that God also has a dream for you. One bigger than anything you could wish for yourself. So big, in fact, that we can't even imagine it. 1 Cor 2, 9. As scripture tells us: ". . . eye has not seen, and ear has not heard . . . what God has prepared for those who love Him . . ." 1 Cor 2, 9. "[W]e are God's children now; what we shall be has not yet been revealed." 1 Jn 3, 2.

All we know is that when God created us, He dreamt that one day we would "shine like the sun". Mt 13, 43; Eph 2, 10; Mt 18, 14. He created us to be, one day, "incorruptible" and "glorious". 1 Cor 15, 42-43. We are called to one day know God "face to face", 1 Cor 13, 12, and on that day God will "wipe every

10

tear from [our] eyes, and there shall be no more death or mourning, wailing or pain . . ." Rev 21, 4.

How's that for a dream? And how's that as a dream for our kids? If we want them to have that one day, let's put the dream before them now so they can see it, know that it's out there for them too, and have a chance at it. Then let's give them the encouragement of seeing their father work toward the same dream, so they'll know it's a worthy dream, deserving of their care and attention, just as it is of ours.

"You may not know what tomorrow holds, but you know who holds tomorrow."

Anonymous

2.

January 6, Feast of the Epiphany

Know It Like It Is

The Dutch are, on statistical average, the tallest people in the world. To anyone with even a passing familiarity with Dutch cuisine, the question is: how is this possible?

I spent a month in Holland on an exchange program, living and eating in Dutch homes around the country. It gave me a pretty good gastronomical snapshot of Dutch culinary habits, and left me with continuing puzzlement as to how the Dutch can grow so tall.

Their hospitality was wonderful. Their food was . . . interesting.

For breakfast, it was plain white bread, buttered—but not toasted—with chocolate sprinkles on top. Where in the United States grocery stores have aisles devoted to breakfast cereal, in the Netherlands they have shelves and shelves full of little boxes with different varieties of sprinkles to shake on top of your white bread and butter in the morning.

For lunch, I had *bitterballen*, a food eaten only in Holland and its former colonies and nowhere else in the world. Apparently it takes an armed garrison to impose a *bitterballen* habit. I'll tell you why: *bitterballen* is minced crawfish rolled in a ball of congealed goo formed from crawfish-gravy, flour, butter and a combustible mix of *hot* spices, all battered and deep fried.

Mmmm. Pass the breath mints, please.

A classic Dutch dinner is raw herring. That's right. Read it again. I said "*raw* herring". Make your mouth water? Well, try it, and it will make your eyes water. Now, I have to admit that these days raw herring is more a matter of sport-eating—a nostalgic once-a-year remembrance of a bygone maritime and fishing heritage—not a regular staple of work-a-day family meals. But it gives you a historical perspective. Just imagine how bad Dutch cookery must have been back in the day if it was actually preferable to eat the herring raw.

The moral of this story is that if you find yourself ordering food in Holland, you better be careful. Which is hard to do, because the Dutch language is close to incomprehensible. From what I could tell there is no Dutch word spelled with less than 10 letters, and they have a consonant to vowel ratio of about 8 to 1. Which is hard on the eyes when you're trying to decipher a menu under the gaze of an impatient waiter.

One day I was at the seaside town of Schraevening, staring at a menu, trying to find meaning in enormous strings of letters thrown down on the page in the seemingly random arrangements comprising Dutch words. Amidst the jumble of consonants, my eyes alit on the word "*frites*". After three weeks in Holland my command of the Dutch language had progressed impressively to the point where I knew that "*frites*" meant "fries". Unfortunately, the word "*frites*" was preceded by something like "*Schlloftenchgosch*" and followed by something like "*chlthigrthrynch*". I didn't know what those meant, but what could it matter? I pointed and ordered.

Big mistake. As a lawyer, I should have known better. The words you understand are never the problem. It's the ones you don't that'll getcha.

What they brought me was a big plate of French fries alright—slathered in mayonnaise and peanut sauce. Together. On the same plate. On the same fries. I humbly suggest that mayonnaise *never* goes with peanut sauce in *any* application, even as engine lubricant.

The rest of the day was long and hungry. What I would have given for some white bread and butter with chocolate sprinkles on top. But a little hunger in Holland taught me a lesson. In this world, we can't pass blind and blissful over the gaping pits of our ignorance, we have to shine light into the dark spaces.

That's especially true with our faith. In *The Weight of Glory*, C. S. Lewis said:

> If our religion is something objective, then we must never avert our eyes from those elements in it which seem puzzling or repellent; for it will be precisely

13

the puzzling or the repellent which conceals what
we do not yet know and need to know.

On *The Journey Home* television program, Scott Hahn and
Marcus Grodi were reflecting on their experiences of conversion to
Catholicism after years of intense Bible study as protestant
ministers:

[Scott Hahn:] . . . I had fun going through the Bible
for about three years and looking at what I
underlined and then noticing what I had not
underlined after fifteen years of bible study and
often times it was more significant to notice what I
had not underlined, what I had ignored, what I had
suppressed, what I was dodging . . . * * * * *

[Marcus Grodi:] What's the underlying reason then
that those weren't underlined?

[Scott Hahn:] Well, I think it's because we tend to
see either what we've experienced or we tend to see
what we've been shown and what we've been
taught. And so, often, our reading is a kind of re-
enforcement of already existing understanding . . . *
* * * * And so you go deeper and deeper and what
you find is you keep seeing over and over again
what you were shown or what you've experienced .
. . * * * * * And then suddenly a few things
happened, a few graces were given, and the scales
began to fall off my eyes.

[Marcus Grodi:] The scales are the great example,
because we—the idea was that we would go almost
like with a clean slate: 'What is the bible teaching
me?' And in reality we didn't do that. We went with
pre-conceived understandings about certain things
and then we would find verses that fit that . . . that's
what shapes the glasses, and everything comes from

14

that, and that's why we would skip and miss verses .
. .

Editing and punctuation added.

The human mind has a tendency to seize on what it already knows and recognizes (or at least what it thinks it knows), and to skip over and ignore what is foreign, what it does not already know or understand. But that doesn't do us much good. If we pick and choose, approaching God with a selective reading, we aren't really coming to know God at all. Instead, we're just projecting our own ideas and our images onto God. Scripture warns us to guard against this tendency: "Every word of God is tested; He is a shield to those who take refuge in Him. Add nothing to His words, lest He reprove you, and you be exposed as a deceiver." Prv 30, 5-6. "In your observance of the commandments of the Lord, your God, which I enjoin upon you, you shall not add to what I command you nor subtract from it." Deut 4, 2. "I warn everyone who hears the prophetic words in this book: if anyone adds to them, God will add to him the plagues described in this book, and if anyone takes away from the words in this prophetic book, God will take away his share in the tree of life and in the holy city described in this book." Rev 22, 18. St. Paul wrote: "As we have said before, and now I say again, if anyone preaches to you a gospel other than the one that you received, let that one be accursed! * * * * * I want you to know, brothers, that the gospel preached by me is not of human origin. For I did not receive it from a human being, nor was I taught it, but it came through a revelation of Jesus Christ." Gal 1, 6-12.
Taking a piecemeal approach to Scripture, or any of the faith passed on to us by the Apostles and preserved in the Church, effectively creates a species of the variant gospel that St. Paul warns against. Which is why we have to stop when we come to those parts of Scripture or our faith that don't seem to jive with us, that we don't like or understand, and work to know them—not avert our eyes. We need to go deeper into those things which are a mystery to us or that we find difficult to accept. Trying to know truth, trying to know God, is a different exercise from trying to conform God and truth to our pre-conceived notions (or even, sometimes, our desires).

15

The Epiphany is a feast celebrating three wise men who set out seeking God. They searched the sky, they followed the signs, and they embarked on a quest to find Him. The magi first looked in a palace, naturally assuming, I suppose, that kings should be sought in palaces. But it was not to be so. This King was like no other, and He was not to be found in the court of Herod or any other earthly potentate. One can only wonder what the magi thought when their quest finally led them to a stable, a dirty cave, and a poor baby laying in an animal's feeding trough.

God has a way of surprising us. The real God may (and probably will) turn out to be different from our thoughts about God—and much greater than our thoughts. So the thing is not to formulate our own version of God, drawn only from our own limited resources, but to step into a larger world and seek to know God as He really is.

Besides, we don't have a choice. Reality is not optional. We can come to know the truth, and therefore be able to make good decisions and live well, or we can order from the menu blind and ignorant. But trying to project our own vision of dietary delight onto reality won't change a peanut-sauce-and-mayonnaise concoction into something scrumptious. If we want the good stuff, we need some understanding. That requires first the willingness to search for reality as it actually exists, to seek to know God as He is, rather than how we think He ought to be. If we can do that, the scales will begin to fall away from our eyes also and we may see things that were always before us, but we never noticed before.

"The task ahead of us is never as great as the Power behind us."

Anonymous

16

3.

Craft Time

You've got to take whatever life throws at you. And if you're a parent, you probably have to wipe it up, too.

Especially when it comes to craft time. Few words can strike more fear into the hearts of parents with young toddlers than "craft time." When the paint is flying and the glue is dripping, things can get a little distressing—particularly for your furniture.

I'm always interested in old parenting "how-to" books from yesteryear, and in one from 1964 called "A Do-It-Yourself Guide to Family Fun and Recreation" by Richard Frisbee, I found this about craft time:

> Creativity involves curiosity, experimentation, exploration. From the parent's point of view, it also involves messes—crayon faces in the wrong places, spilled paint and chemicals, widely strewn paper and cloth scraps—and noise. The natural reaction is to put a stop to it.

Some parents I know just refuse to do crafts at home. Probably because they've seen our carpets. Because in our family, we love drippy, sparkly, sticky, gooey, colorful old craft time. We are frequent crafters, and our multi-colored kid's crafting table proudly bears the mark of many a happy, creative afternoon. At least once a day, sometimes twice or even thrice, our older daughter will say: "I want to do a craft." The one year old simply exclaims: "Craft!" And so we delve into our supply of glue and glitter; string and scissors; buttons, bows, and "who-knows" (which are all the little bits of odd things saved for 'who-knows-what,' since you just never know when you might need something exactly like that), and begin creating.

Each time we do, a new mystery is afoot. Because no matter what our intentions at the outset, we can never be sure where our crafting will take us. I've finally learned, after years of collecting data in the wild, that starting a new craft means embarking on a journey into the unknown. And strangely, the unexpected twists and turns of the creative process used to be just about as stress inducing as the mess potential. Spills I learned to anticipate (more or less), and take appropriate advanced precautions to mediate the damage. With sponges at the ready and only washable paints deployed at the table, and an old dumpster-fodder throw rug protecting the floor, Daddy could deal with most vicissitudes of crafting's dirty side. But I've never figured how to predict the final destination of the crafting odyssey once we set out on the road of pre-school creativity.

My best laid plans, my most carefully assembled supplies, my most assiduously detailed step-by-step road map for craft completion, rarely do any of them bare much resemblance to the craft as it actually unfolds in the real world.

Take our Bear Caves. Our girls love the "Big Bear, Little Bear" books by Waddell and Firth. So, I thought, why not make our own bear caves out of cardboard boxes? First we'd scour the park for little pebbles, then save some cardboard boxes from packages that come in the mail, and glue the stones onto the boxes. We'd cut flaps out of the boxes for doors and windows, and glue sticks on our diminutive portals of ingress and egress for a little natural-wood charm to offset the austerity of our stone walls. In the end, we'd have beautifully rustic little bear caves we could decorate with furniture made from spools of thread, those little three-legged plastic tables that come in pizza delivery boxes, and stamps for pictures on the wall.

Things started well. We had great fun amassing a pyramid of pebbles in the park. Back at home the girls loved squeezing the tubes of glue as hard as they could and spreading the gooey gunk all over the boxes. Next we started pressing our little stones into the glue. So far, so good. All was going according to plan and we had pleasantly rugged mini-grizzly caverns in the early stages of gestation.

But craft time is fluid and dynamic, not static. What you see one moment changes the next. Liz, our older daughter, put

18

down her little handful of pebbles and ran off. She came back bearing a bucket of "jewels"—colored glass stones we acquired to serve as fairy treasures for another craft.

"Look how pretty these are on my bear cave!" Liz enthused as she arranged them onto the glue of her cave walls. Then she actually started removing the park stones that were already stuck onto the cardboard and replacing them with her fairy jewels. Brown and grey rock gave way to shiny bits of pink and lavender.

Soon her little sister joined in the act, retrieving a jar of marbles to add a splash of color to her Bear Cave. Next, out came their plastic bracelet-making beads and suddenly our bear abodes sparkled with peach-colored plastic butterflies and fuchsia stars. My rough-hued vision of wilderness crafting faded before a burgeoning panoply of flowers and jewels spread in a pastel harmony of pinks and purples, salmon and sky-blue, like a princess rainbow across the walls of the Bear Caves.

I found all this very disconcerting. Bear caves are supposed to be dens for fearsome, shaggy beasts of tooth and claw that lumber through forests primeval and ramble the rocky heights of untamed mountains. There are no gems or jewels, hearts or butterflies on bear caves. Only sticks and stones: black, brown, and gray. Some natural wood accents on the doors and windows are acceptable. But definitely no lavender or fuchsia.

Our whole project was transmogrifying from a bear cave into Tinkerbell's summer cottage.

Times like these I struggle to stay my hand. I have to check a tendency to want to force things to adhere to my own preconceived script. In battling this desire to control and mold, to remake the world in my own image, craft time has become for me one of the many little homilies of the Domestic Church. It's been a lesson in what Scripture tells us: "In his mind a man plans his course, but the Lord directs his steps." Prv 16, 9.

After all, the thing with crafting is the doing. It's the exercise of imagination and motor skills. Learning to overcome obstacles and find a way to get things done. Developing foresight, expanding the event horizon beyond the next five minutes and starting to realize that bigger things can be achieved with applied effort over a period of days, or even weeks. And of course, crafts are about fun: engaging the world of God's creation, exploring, and getting your hands dirty.

And those very skills: creativity, finding a way to get things done, imagination and inspiration, getting your hands dirty, just *doing*, are the very elements of the unexpected that lead away from Daddy's preconceived notions into uncharted waters.

As it is with crafts, so it is with life. Things don't always (or maybe I should say "often") go as we expect. Life is a journey into unexplored territory, and we've got to deal with the surprising twists and turns as they come, clean-up the inevitable spills along the way, and realize we're not really in control. The very things that make a life well-lived and worth living are themselves elements of the unexpected, leading us away from the courses we plot for ourselves and out onto the grand pilgrimage into the unknown that God calls us to. When we are willing to leave the confines of our own ways and step into that larger unknown, wonderful surprises await us, like when we set out seeking only stones and instead find beautiful jewels.

Give me patience when little hands,
Tug at me with small demands
Give me gentle words and smiling eyes
And keep my lips from sharp replies,
So in years to come when my house is still
Beautiful memories it's rooms may fill.

Anonymous

4.

A Mystery Unfolds

God, I've found, utilizes a "just-in-time" operational model. And He chooses the most unexpected vendors and suppliers, mixing them together in unforeseeable combinations. As this mystery story reveals.

It's a mystery that begins with a love of books, is leavened with some good old-fashioned cheapness, and ends with a Black Day turned Red, thanks to the mediation of a dead Bishop, a priest I never met, the Unknown Instigator, and the Unknowing Messenger.

First the love books. I love to read them, to feel them in my hands, I even love the smell of books. I think it's a natural affinity inborn to all men—as proven by my 16 month old daughter. She can't read, but she loves to pull books off our shelves and run around the house with them, flipping through the pages. They end up in the oddest places, which is usually cute, like when you find a book she particularly loves sitting next to the milk in the refrigerator. But it's not so cute when you find them floating in the bath tub. The hazards of a bibliophile's life with small children.

I also love to acquire books. This is where the cheapness plays its part. Growing up one of eight children, I developed a large respect for the value of small pennies. But when it comes to books, I'm aided by the dear dead Bishop of this story: The Most Reverend Archbishop John Ireland. Born in Ireland, educated in France, he served as a Chaplain in the Civil War and eventually became the first Archbishop of St. Paul, Minnesota. A colonizer, he founded (or helped found) more than a dozen towns in the American West, and a host of institutions in St. Paul and around the country, including: The Catholic University of America (CUA) in Washington, D.C. (where my wife went to college), St. Thomas University (which brought my wife and I to St. Paul), and, in 1894, the St. Paul Seminary (which numbers among its illustrious graduates 31 bishops and counting, including Archbishop Fulton Sheen, who also taught philosophy at CUA for 24 years).

As part of the St. Paul Seminary, Archbishop Ireland also founded what is now known as the Archbishop Ireland Memorial Library. It's one of my favorite libraries. The reading room is magnificent: twenty foot ceilings, long wooden tables, stained glass windows, shelf-tops adorned with busts in marble and bronze, displays of archaeological finds from the ancient Mediterranean scattered hither and yon, Medieval illustrated sheet music and pictures of popes hanging on the walls—it's a neat place. The library also has a friendly staff, a microwave, free Wi-Fi, and a quirkiness I appreciate. For example, on the landing leading to the second floor there's a table with a chess game set-up. Two empty chairs face each other across the chess board, with a little cardboard sign pointed at one chair that reads "Your move." You're welcome to take the empty seat and make the next move. Then you turn the sign around to face the other chair and wait until you come back again to see how the game has developed.

They also have a special tradition, started by the Unknown Instigator. Here the mystery progresses. As a Seminary library, the collections and patrons of the Ireland lean heavily toward the religious. An unknown person, sometime long ago, started tucking prayer cards into books when returning them to the library. Whoever it was, they had a knack for evangelization. The idea caught on and now the Ireland Library has thousands of prayer cards. And here again we see an example of why I love the Ireland. The staff, aware that they had a rare and special, if unlooked for, treasure, decided to preserve the prayer cards by digitizing them. Images of the cards that have already been scanned are posted on the library's web-site. Pretty cool.

But above all, I love the Ireland for the books. And not just the ones in their collections, but also the ones they give away. That's right, the Ireland not only holds books, it also gives them away. It's a small library with limited space, so they are constantly combing through the stacks, pulling out the old to make room for the new. The culled stock goes first to the sale table, where a hard-back sells for $1.00 and paperbacks for 50 cents. Things lingering too long on the sale table make a final stop at the freebie-cart.

Located just inside the front door, under a smiling bronze bust of Archbishop Ireland, a sign above the cart reads: "Free—Help yourself to any of the books or materials on this cart."

On the venerable freebie-cart I've found many a treasure. So many, in fact, that my wife put me under orders to slow the pace of acquisitions. Free or no, she noted, our family library had to recognize the same constraints of spatial reality that compelled the Ireland to discard the books in the first place—and I was given to understand in no uncertain terms that the refrigerator was not a viable option for additional book storage capacity.

One of those treasures from the Ireland came in handy on my Black Day. The Romans considered certain days "Black Days"—days so bad you were forbidden from performing any public business, religious ceremonies, or even private business on them. Black Days were, and are, pretty bad—and on the day this mystery unfolded I was experiencing my own.

I was in the kitchen getting our daughter's lunch ready, mulling over in my mind (with particular fervor and bulldog tenacity) the grievous woes of the world. Well, not so much the woes of the *whole* wide world as the problems of one small subset of the world, namely: me.

I stood there ruminating on my burdens, cutting carrots with a vengeance—Chop! Chop!—and scowling like Ebenezer Scrooge after Bob Cratchit asked for a second lump of coal, when our daughter walked in. She was holding a little slip of paper in her hand. She toddled up to me and held the paper out.

I stopped what I was doing and looked down at her.

"Hi Love," I said, "how are you doing?"

"Hi-ya!" she answered, reaching the paper up to me.

"What's this?" I asked, bending down to look at it.

She gave it to me, then ran off, beaming with satisfaction at having successfully completed her delivery.

It was an old prayer card from the 1930's, which began:

The Apostolate of Smiling

Just a Little Smile on Your Lips
    Cheers your heart

Keeps you in good humor
Preserves peace in your soul
Promotes your health
Beautifies your face
Induces kindly thoughts
Inspires kindly deeds.

SMILE TO YOURSELF . . .
until you notice that your constant seriousness, or
even severity, has vanished.

SMILE TO YOURSELF . . .
until you have warmed your own heart with the
sunshine of your cheery countenance. Then . . .
Go out—and radiate your smile.

THAT SMILE . . .
has work to do—work to do for God.

* * * * *

That's just an excerpt, but I read the whole thing. It's good.
Written by a certain Father Bruno Hagspiel, S.V.D., about whom I
knew nothing (an internet search told me he was born in "West
Prussia" in 1885 and emigrated to the United States in 1910), it's a
sort of Litany of Smiling, a cross between an exhortation and a
prayer, the kind of thing Norman Vincent Peale might have written
if he'd been a Dominican.

The Unknowing Messenger, unable even to read, had just
delivered a message from a priest I never met. Transmitted via the
prayer-card tradition started by the Unknown Instigator and made
possible by the dead Bishop's founding of a library, it was brought
by a love of books (combined with cheapness) into the range of a
one-year-old's curious hands, to be conveyed to me at the very
moment I needed that message.

I smiled.

I had to. How can you not when something like that
happens? Besides, I figured I better. As Pope John Paul II said:
"In the designs of Providence there are no mere coincidences," and

the message I got was clear. I didn't see how forcing a fake smile on my face could make any difference when I was wrestling with dark thoughts in my breast, but no one asked my opinion—I just got the message that I had better smile. So I did.

It worked!

I don't know how or why, but it really did cheer my heart. And I found that once the dark spell of gloom is pierced, even by the merest pin-prick of light, it bursts like a balloon. With a snap of the fingers, my Black Day was transformed into a Red Letter Day (which comes from medieval church calendars, that marked Saints Days and other special days in red letters). And the letters spelled: S-M-I-L-E.

It also helped me realize the importance of vocations. Certainly the vocations of priests and other professed religious, who were among the main actors in my personal drama. But also us laymen, who have our own missions as well. God's work needs doing, and He calls on each of us to contribute our labors, mighty or meager as they may be. At times, that can be hard to remember—especially when it seems we have only a bit part in the great spectacle of life and the universe. But if our personal part sometimes seems insignificant, that's only because we're not given to see all the fruits that grow from our contribution to the grand pitch-in of Creation and Salvation. Bishop Ireland, Father Hagspiel, the Unknown Instigator—even the Unknowing Messenger—none of them knew how they impacted the life of one new father, and through that father a whole family—a family whose existence they never even knew of (well, except the Unknowing Messenger; as a member of the family, she knew about that).

As Aslan says in *The Horse and His Boy*, "I am telling you your story, not hers. No one is told any story but their own." The mystery of how our own story will alter the stories of others, of how all the threads intertwine and combine together to form a grand tapestry, isn't ours to know. Following the line of just one strand, the design of the whole can't be perceived. To see that requires standing back to view the entire tapestry at once. But confined as we are to the perspective of our own life alone, our own limited space and time, we just can't see the whole design. It's too vast. Besides, even if there were some mystic cosmic flash, some sparkling instant of transcendence that somehow allowed us to see it all together in its entirety at one time, we humans are far too finite a creature to take it in.

But then, we don't need to. What's important is just to know that we have work to do, and that work counts. As George Weigel wrote in *Letters to a Young Catholic*: "*There is purpose in the world, divine purpose.*" (Emphasis in original.) Even if we can't know all the effects our work has, we can know that it is affective. It matters. For good or ill, what we do will reach out beyond ourselves, beyond our own limited perception and knowledge, even beyond our own place and time. So if a moment comes when you find yourself discouraged, think about a mystery, the mystery of how God uses the most unlikely instruments— including even you and me—in the most unforeseeable combinations, to shape the world in ways we can't imagine. And smile.

"When we do the best we can, we never know what miracles await."

Helen Keller

5.

Litany of the Everyday

In our family we observe a common Catholic tradition: whenever we hear a siren, we say a Hail Mary, "for whoever is in need and for the first responders."

Since we live just a few blocks from a fire station, we get lots of practice in this devotion.

Which also affords our daughter Liz, now two years old, plenty of opportunity to indulge her new passion: she loves reciting prayer lists as long as your arm. The longer, the better, and once she gets started it's hard to stop her.

It's my own fault, really. During the intention part of our nightly family prayers we usually run down the names of everyone in the family to pray for them. I've got seven siblings, all of them married and most with kids. Plus a wonderful grandmother still living, scores of aunts and uncles and cousins, and of course we have the dearly departed to remember in prayer, so it makes for a sizeable list even before we get to my wife's side of the family.

As a result, Liz has developed the idea that prayer intentions should come in epic, unroll-the-scroll size lists. I have to concede that there's a certain logic to her approach. With a universe of need out there, why confine yourself to just one or two prayer intentions? But it also means that our dinners now start something like this:

"Bless us O Lord, and these Thy gifts . . ."

"And Harry," Liz interjects.

"And bless Harry," I'll say, then continue: "from thy bounty . . ."

"And Melissa," Liz says.

I nod my head. "And please bless Melissa, also" and then continue: "through Christ Our Lord . . ."

"And Grandpa," Liz chimes in.

"And Grandpa," I agree.

And when I see Liz drawing breath and preparing to open her mouth again, I dart in with a fast "Amen." It's a tactic I use sometimes to surprise her—the prayer equivalent of a quick-snap in football—and bring proceedings to a close before she can continue her list. I know, it sounds bad—cutting-off the prayers of a child. Whoever heard of a parenting handbook of strategies to curb kinder piety? But sometimes I have to, or our family might never eat a hot meal again.

The same thing happens with our Hail Mary's when we hear a siren. What should be a quick 40 second prayer can grow to a catalogue of intentions rivaling the Federal Budget in volume.

So it was the other day when I got Liz after her nap. I changed her diaper and was holding her in the brown easy-chair—the Bear Chair, as it's been dubbed ever since the book *Can't You Sleep Little Bear?* first made its entrance into our pre-bed-time reading rotation. Liz likes a cuddle in the Bear Chair after her nap and we were deep in our post-slumber snuggle when we heard a siren.

Liz looked up at me.

"Hail Mary, Daddy," she instructed.

"You're right, Honey," I agreed.

I made the sign of the cross, and began our prayer.

Liz watched intently through the Hail Mary, alert for her opening, wary lest Daddy try a quick-snap Amen. As soon as the words "and the first responders" left my lips, she sprang into the opening, proclaiming: "And for the hammer!"

We have a rule that we don't pray for inanimate objects, but we can thank the Lord for them, so I said: "And thank you Jesus for our hammer."

"And coping saw," Liz said, nodding solemnly. (We had been exploring the tool chest earlier, and saw that it was good, so tools were much on her mind.)

"And thank you Jesus for our coping saw."

Now she was in her stride and out poured a list of all the things that have fascinated or delighted a two-year old as of late, and we thanked Jesus for each:

Closets (fun to hide in).

Clothes (especially scooped into a pile on the floor for playing in).

Couch (great for jumping on).

Sweatshirt (cozy).

Coke (delicious).

Mountain Dew (even more delicious).

And so on, and so on, and so on. I resigned myself to Liz's extensive Litany of the Everyday, sure that she'll be one of the few people who actually enjoy the genealogical "begat" sections of the Bible. My head lolled back on the Bear Chair as I intoned "Thank you Jesus for . . ." an assortment of items ranging from dollies to donuts. Then, just as my thoughts started to wander, Liz hit me with a zinger: "Thank you for Liz being born."

I sat up in the Bear Chair. It was Liz's birthday a few weeks before, and on her birthday we had thanked God for giving us the gift of her. Ever since her birthday balloon-blowing and Happy-Birthday-singing had been favorite games, so I knew the candles and cake and other festive trappings had been appreciated, but I didn't realize the prayer in thanks of herself had also made an impression.

"And thank you Jesus for the gift of Liz," I said, not without a little more huskiness in my voice than usual.

I was also struck with a realization from Liz's juxtaposition of the extraordinary with the ordinary. Snuggling drowsy and cozy with my daughter in the Bear Chair, I saw that I was probably like a lot of the folks in the crowd of the 5,000 (Mt 14, 13-21) and the 4,000 (Mt 15, 32-39) receiving loaves and fishes without fully appreciating the gifts placed in my hands.

It's a matter of perspective. The multiplication of the loaves and fishes is always told from the insiders' point of view, the twelve apostles, those with a front-row seat who were in the know and fully apprised of the audacious facts—that Jesus proposed to feed a vast multitude with a handful of fish and a few loaves of bread.

The apostles knew full well what was happening. It was they who had counted their meager stores and told Jesus there was no way they could feed all the people with what little they had. Not even with 200 days wages could they feed the vast crowd assembled there in a deserted wilderness. And it was the apostles who Jesus charged with feeding this crowd, telling the apostles to have the throngs seat themselves on the ground in companies. The apostles obeyed, and the people did too, sitting in groups of 50 or 100. Jesus blessed the food, broke it, and gave it to the apostles to distribute.

So the apostles were acutely aware of what was happening, and when they collected baskets full of scraps after all the people had eaten their fill, the Apostles knew what a miracle had been wrought in their in presence.

But what about the people out there sitting on the ground? They weren't given any announcement about what was happening. No one ascended a raised dais with clanging gongs and shouted to the multitude: "Prepare to be dazzled as the amazing Jesus multiplies loaves and fishes before your very eyes!" For them, the people out there sitting on the ground, it was just "Pass the fish and bread, please."

Deep in the crowd were probably plenty of folks with no idea what was going on with the loaves and the fishes. I wonder how many stopped to ask themselves, "Hey, we're way out here in the wilderness, a long way from town, and I haven't seen any catering company setting-up cooking fires, so where did all this food come from? How did these guys cart enough bread and fish out here to feed all these people, with no advanced notice or planning?" Or how many just ate, without ever considering the source of their bounty?

All I know is that one member of the modern throng, sitting in a Bear Chair holding a little girl who still had the good sense to look on everyday things with the wonder and gratitude they deserve, had only been eating his fill without really considering the source of his bounty. As with the loaves and fishes, there's no clamor of fanfare accompanying the ordinary, everyday blessings God bestows on us, nothing to remind us just how extraordinary His everyday gifts really are. We just get the blessings.

It made me think of something I heard Mother Angelica say once on EWTN. Mother Angelica said, "If someone hands you a piece of cherry pie, say 'Thank You, Jesus.'" Now that's a good perspective on the reality of where we stand in this world. I would only add, per Liz, that while you're at it, tell Him thanks for the coping saw, too.

6.

Corn Jobs

My wife and I were at the home of another married couple for dinner. While a roast finished cooking, we sat around the table talking and eating salad. When the oven timer rang, the wife turned to her husband and said, "That's a corn job."

The husband got up and went to the kitchen. He pulled the roast out of the oven and carved it. When he brought it to the table, there was a beautiful roasted beast . . . but no corn.

"Didn't you say this was a corn job?" my wife asked.

Our hosts looked at each other and laughed.

"Yes," the husband said. "That comes from when we were first married."

They told us that, like many newly married couples, it took them a little time to work out a division of labor. About six months after their wedding, when they were still sorting through that process, it was a summer day and they were driving up to the lake. Produce stands spring up along the country roads in the summer, and they decided to stop at one for some corn. They pulled over on the side of the road near a cute little produce stand, painted red with a yellow awning.

And there they sat.

Neither reached for the door, neither made any move to get out of the car and go get the corn.

Minutes passed.

Still, they waited, each sitting and looking straight ahead out the windshield.

"Well," the husband finally asked, "aren't you going to get the corn?"

"Aren't *you* going to get the corn?" the wife replied.

"In my family, my Mom always got the corn."

"Well in my family, my Dad always got the corn."

31

And so they sat in their car on the side of the road and began hashing out who would get the corn in *their* family. While each of them came from a family of origin, they were beginning to realize that "my family" now meant something different: the new family they had founded together. And they had to work out for themselves how things operated in this newly constituted family. In the end, it was determined that, for their family, the husband would get the corn at roadside stands.

"Ever since," the husband concluded, "we call husband jobs 'corn jobs.'"

My wife and I could relate. There is certainly no shortage of work in a family, especially when you have kids. You need all the dogs pulling the sled to get across the tundra. Some jobs can be allocated by mutual accord. For others, training and predilection help the delegation. If one spouse is an accountant, it makes sense for them to do the family taxes. Still other jobs go to one spouse or another as a matter of necessity. My wife can't reach the top shelf of our pantry, so that's where I stash the Twinkies.

Just kidding, of course. (At least as far as she knows.) And I know it's a small example, but it points to something true: certain jobs Daddy has to do. Certain jobs *only* Daddy can do. By necessity some things are "corn jobs."

I saw this in an unexpected place: a reading at mass of a Bible story I had heard many times before. With long familiar Bible passages, my mind tends to wander. For the stories that make it into the Sunday readings every year, I remember them, I've heard plenty of homilies on them, and I figure I already know "the lesson." Only now that I'm married and have kids, I'm discovering a lot of new things I never noticed before.

So it was with the story of Jesus bringing the synagogue officials daughter to life in Mark's Gospel. Mk 5, 21-24, 35-43. When Jesus arrived, the little girl was already dead and a crowd of mourners filled the house. Of all the gathered people, the Bible tells us that Jesus "put them all out." Mk 5, 40. Then, "He took along the child's father and mother and those who were with him [the apostles Peter, James and John] and entered the room where the child was." Mk 5, 40. Jesus took the girl by the hand and restored her to life. Mk 5, 43. Jesus then "said that she should be given something to eat." Mk 5, 43.

The message I always associated with this passage was the importance of faith, and that message is certainly evident. But what struck me now was that Jesus called both the mother *and* father to be present when life was given to the child. Everyone else was sent out. Neighbors, friends, relatives, *everyone else* among the mourners—none of them were a substitute for the mother, or the father. When life is given to a child, it is both the mother and the father who are called, in and through and with the Church (which is the body of Christ), evident here in Peter, James and John. Then, once Jesus had given life to the child, He charged them to feed her: both the mother and father are given the task of caring for and sustaining the child.

As a father, I saw in this Scripture the importance of the fatherly vocation. In our modern culture, the depiction of fatherhood sometimes has a sense of disposability about it. As though the role of the father in the family is ancillary, or even optional. Jesus shows us otherwise. Jesus called both the mother and father when life was given to the child, and both the mother and father were charged with feeding the child—with the ongoing nurture and care of the life given by God. The Bible is showing us that the role of the father is not disposable or optional or something that can be delegated to another.

The Church continues to stress the importance of fathers in the life of their children and families. Peter was present when Jesus gave life to the child in Mark's Gospel, and Peter's successor, Saint John Paul II—John Paul the Great—noted the importance of strong fatherhood in *Familiaris Consortio*, writing that "where social and cultural conditions so easily encourage a father to be less concerned with his family . . . efforts must be made to restore socially the conviction that the place and task of the father in and for the family is of unique and irreplaceable importance."

The vocation of fatherhood is a calling from God Himself, Who entrusts His children to us for a time, and charges us with caring for them. Just think about that: God trusts *us* with *His* children—His children who He created to one day shine like the sun in Heaven for all eternity. Mt 13, 43. And God has put us in their lives to protect and nurture those children and help get them there. When that sinks in we can begin to realize the divine nature of the responsibility He's given us and the nobility of our calling.

Fatherhood means corn jobs, for sure. It is definitely a vocation of service, of denying oneself in favor of others. And sometimes amid the constant demands of work and diapers, sleepless nights with sick children, or the evolving challenges that come as kids grow older, we can lose sight of the true nature of our fatherly calling. It's good to remember amid the occasionally overwhelming welter of mundane details that comes with fatherhood that it's all part of a work of divine importance, and we have been called to it by Jesus Christ Himself.

"Have patience with all things, but chiefly have patience with yourself. Do not lose courage in considering your own imperfections but instantly set about remedying them—every day begin the task anew."

St. Francis De Sales

7.

Valentine's Day

Paths that Cross

You never know who you might meet. Sometimes I wish I could see my path plotted on a map in bright red like in the Indiana Jones movies—a dotted line showing everywhere I've been in my life. Then I want to cross-reference my path against the paths of others, to see who was where, when. Is there an App for that?

My wife and I were with friends one evening and the talk turned to churches. First it was architecture: old-style churches versus modern "theatre" churches built in the round. Small local parish churches versus monumental tourist attraction basilicas. Which led to a discussion of different parish cultures, like choirs in traditional robes singing from a loft in the back of the church, or guitars and keyboards up front.

Which led us eventually to talking pastors and homilies. I recounted one of my favorite homily stories. It was years ago, before kids, even before I met my wife. I was at a local parish that had a great young priest who was a fantastic homilist. He always started with humor, and then once he got you laughing—when he knew you were listening—he'd hit you with the serious stuff.

Along with being really funny, he had a great cadence and sense of timing for building to a dramatic climax. He was in full force this particular Sunday. All eyes were fixed on him at the pulpit, the congregation hanging on every word, as he reached his crescendo.

"God is calling you," he said, "if you will but listen . . . *Listen*, and *you* will *hear* God's call . . ." he paused, the entire church perfectly still, everyone on the edge of their pew, waiting for the next words, when into that pregnant silence . . .

Ring! Ring!

35

A cell phone rang out: blaring, loud, shattering the silence and breaking the spell.

Heads turned. Murmurs and the rustlings of shifting bodies rippled through the congregation.

Father held up his hands to regain everyone's attention, and when all eyes were again on him, he declared: "That was not a plant! I did not plan that!"

The whole church broke out in an uproar of laughter.

As I was telling the story and got to the part about the cell phone, my wife sat up. After I told Father's punch-line, she interrupted: "Was that at St. Pius the Tenth?" she asked.

"Yeah," I answered.

"Father Dan Scheidt? The 5:30 summer mass?"

"Yeah."

"I was at that mass!" she said. "I can't believe it! I was there when that happened! Do you think we saw each other?"

"We must have," I said. "The church isn't that big."

"It's so weird!" she said. "We were both there, and didn't even know each other!"

We cross paths with a lot of interesting people in life. Often there is much more to the people we meet than we suspect, or will ever have the chance of coming to know. I thought about that when I heard the words from Scripture: "Do not neglect hospitality, for through it some have unknowingly entertained angels." Heb 13, 2. You just never know who you are meeting.

And even if the person you meet is not an angel, you never know what that person may become. The parable of the rich man and Lazarus in the Gospel of Luke tells us that the poor man laying in the street, hungry and covered with sores, may one day be in paradise walking with Abraham. Lk 16, 20. He may one day "shine like the sun," Mt 13, 43, Eph 2, 10, Mt 18, 14, and be "incorruptible" and "glorious." 1 Cor 15, 42-43. As C.S. Lewis put it in *The Weight of Glory*, you have never met an ordinary person, because: "There are no *ordinary* people. You have never talked to a mere mortal. Nations, cultures, arts, civilizations – these are mortal, and their life is to ours as the life of a gnat. But it is immortals whom we joke with, work with, marry . . ."

It's a strange thing to realize. At least when it comes to others. I mean, considering myself, of course I know it. It just seems intuitive. But that guy who cuts me off in traffic? The hordes of people waiting in line at the license branch when I just need to renew my plates? Or that demanding client who calls at 4:55 p.m. when I'm all packed-up and ready to head home from work?

Pope Benedict said: "Each of us is the result of a thought of God. Each of us is willed, each of us is loved, each of us is necessary."

It's a good thing to remember when we feel like the dotted red lines from other people's paths are cutting us off, clogging things up or blocking our way. Those moments may just be our chance to show hospitality. And you really never can tell who you might be extending hospitality to, what they will become, or when or where your paths might cross again. You might even find your own dotted line joining theirs in the merging of marriage. And for us parents, that includes those whose own paths start with ours: our children. We don't really know who our children are, or what they may become.

Maybe that's why every once in a while God sends us a friendly little reminder, through Scripture and His other messengers, even those bearing cell phones, to treat others as children of God, because that's what they are—starting with those in our own home.

"Kind words can be short and easy to speak, but their echoes are truly endless."

Mother Theresa

8.

Marked on Ash Wednesday

For Ash Wednesday, my wife and I took the kids to mass at Fulton Sheen's old seminary: the St. Paul Seminary in St. Paul, MN. Located on bluffs above the Mississippi River, with a fine view of the river and the Minneapolis skyline across the water, it has a neat old church with beautiful stone columns, frescoes and stained glass windows.

But before you can get into the church, you have to sign in with the Seminary receptionist. Negotiating our super-long double-stroller through the glass doors, I steered toward the welcome counter—and was startled when the receptionist looked up at us. A cross of black ashes was on her forehead. I knew it was Ash Wednesday, and obviously the receptionist had already been to mass, but it's still arresting to see someone with that cross of black ashes right in the middle of their forehead. "Quite out of the everyday," as Reverend Mosby says in *The Parent Trap*.

After mass, I took our kids on a round of errands: donuts at a local bakery, the bank, and finally the library. At each stop, our presence was similarly arresting to those we encountered. And every year it surprises me. After the Ash Wednesday mass, when I'm out and about pursuing my normal routine, I tend to forget about the ashes on my own forehead. Until I notice people gazing intently at me. Then, even accounting for my dynamic personality and natural charisma, I always end up wondering, "What's up with everyone today?" The extra attention seems odd—until I remember that I too am marked: it's that cross of black ashes on my own forehead. It gets people's attention.

Which is fitting. It's the mark of a Christian, and it is arresting. It tells us about our future—first that we have a future: we are meant for something more, something greater than this

38

limited and fallen existence in this fallen world. Now we are poor banished Children of Eve in this valley of tears, but humankind was not always so, it was not meant to be so, and we will not always be so.

That is why, Jeff Cavins said in *The Great Adventure* Bible study, God sent an angel to guard the Tree of Life after Adam and Eve's sin and fall from grace. Not as punishment, but as protection—to ensure that Adam and Eve would not eat of the Tree of Life and become trapped forever in their corrupted state in a compromised world.

Adam and Eve were not meant to continue indefinitely in their fallen condition, and neither are we. God has something more in store for us than simply this present existence extended into perpetuity. So it is that Saint Augustine asked: "When you have learned that you are immortal – will that be enough for you? It will be something great; but it is too little for me." (quoted by Josef Pieper in *Death and Immortality*, taken from St. Augustine, *Soliloquia* II, 1.)

We are all called to a transcendence and transformation that begins now on this side of the veil, but is completed only on the other side of "from ashes to ashes, and dust to dust."

"Life includes dying, but life does not include death," wrote Father Richard John Neuhaus in *As I Lay Dying*. Father George Rutler, in his audio series *Crisis in Culture*, said "death [is] a deeper mystery than a mere tragedy." Rather, "God is working His purpose out through death." As Father Rutler explained, "we're called through death."

In the First Letter to the Corinthians, St. Paul tells us something of what we are "called through death" to:

> Behold, I tell you a mystery. We shall not all fall asleep, but we will all be changed, in an instant, in the blink of an eye, at the last trumpet. For the trumpet will sound, the dead will be raised incorruptible, and we shall be changed. For that which is corruptible must clothe itself with incorruptibility, and that which is mortal must clothe itself with immortality. 1 Cor 15, 51-53.

One day, we shall be made "glorious" (1 Cor 15, 42), to "shine like the sun". Mt 13, 43; Eph 2, 10; Mt 18, 14.

And it is not just us, St. Paul says, but also "creation awaits with eager expectation the revelation of the children of God; for creation was made subject to futility, not of its own accord but because of the one who subjected it, in hope that creation itself would be set free from slavery to corruption and share in the glorious freedom of the children of God." Rom 8, 18-21.

No wonder the cross of ashes gets so much attention. It's a startling sign of the unexpected possibilities awaiting us, possibilities greater than we could have hoped for ourselves. The mark of a Christian is that he has a future. And paradoxical as it may seem, that future lies through the crucifixion and death commemorated so physically by a cross of ashes pressed upon our flesh on Ash Wednesday.

"And what if somebody did something?"

Father Guiseppe "Pino" Puglisi, Blessed, Martyr, gunned down
Sept. 15, 1993 in Sicily, Italy.

Father Pino would often ask this rhetorical question when people talked about the problems of Sicily, with its rampant crime, corruption, oppression, and poverty.

"We have said: we want to create a different world," he remarked. "Let us strive then to create a climate of honesty, of righteousness, of justice, which means the fulfillment of what pleases God."

Father Pino was assassinated by the mafia.

Quotes and information taken from Edward Pentin, "Murdered by the Mafia, Honored by the Church," *National Catholic Register*, 7/17/12.

9

Second Week of Lent

Beautiful Sleep

Sleep. Beautiful, blissful, blessed sleep. How I love it so . . . how I miss it so! Homer tells us that "the gift of sleep" is "sweet" and that sleep will "speedily free [us] from toilsome weariness." Jeremiah says ". . . my sleep was pleasant to me." Jer 31, 26. Mine was, too, back in the days B.C. ("Before Children").

We big people love sleep, we can't get enough of it. Our problem is trying to wake up in the morning. We want to keep on sleeping and sleeping. There was a guy in college who just couldn't wake up. He set an alarm in vain. He would routinely turn it off in his sleep without ever waking up—and he slept in a loft.

He would climb down from the loft, turn off the alarm, and climb back into bed, all without waking. He had to start putting his alarm in a corner on the other side of the room and arraying an obstacle course between his bed and the clock. He blocked the path with his bike, a skateboard, a basketball, golf clubs, etc., and at the end of this trail of perils he put his laundry basket over the alarm clock. All in the hopes that he would actually wake up in the process of negotiating his way through these hazards (hopefully without breaking a leg). It still didn't work all the time. One morning I heard him yelling, but not from banging his shins. He had dreamed that he was defusing a bomb. The good news was that in his dream he successfully averted an explosion. The bad news was that what he had actually defused was his alarm clock, and then he overslept a class.

Our daughter was born eight months ago and I can count the number of times I've slept through the night since then: once. I know, because my wife won't let me forget. I woke up in the morning after that one blissful night of uninterrupted slumber feeling refreshed, with a sparkle in my eye and a spring in my step.

"That was amazing," I told my wife. "Liz slept all night without waking up."

My wife looked at me through bleary, blood-shot eyes and answered: "No, *you* slept all night without waking up."

Sorry, Honey. But it was nice.

Most nights I feel like my sister Rachel did back when we were kids. One night, when she was seven, Rachel walked into the room shared by my brothers John and Mark. John and Mark were 17 and 16 at the time, and they were blaring rock music and lifting weights at 1 a.m. (Why not? Who doesn't want to lift weights to loud rock music at 1 a.m.?) I was there, too, because of course as a little brother I thought John and Mark were about as cool as you could get (and they are, really).

Rachel walked in and asked: "Could you turn the music up please?"

John paused with a barbell half-hoisted.

"What?" he asked. "You want me to turn it *up*?"

"Yeah," Rachel said sweetly in a sleepy little voice. "I don't think they can hear it in Japan yet."

Well, our daughter must be on the road to being as cool as John and Mark, because she thinks the wee small hours of the night are a great time to be up and active. I've found it to be the hardest part of being a new parent: getting up at 1 a.m. . . . and 3 a.m. . . . and 5 a.m. Then pacing the floor in the dark, hour after hour, trying to induce somnolence in our progeny.

Mornings after a night like that are brutal. The world doesn't give you a pass because your kids kept you up all night. Everything continues apace in its hectic way and expects you to keep up just as if you spent the night floating peacefully on the soft clouds of dreamland. You've still got to get up and get to work, and feed those very same fussy little buggers who kept you up all night, and get the trash to the curb, and pack lunch, and . . . well, you know the rest. All the ever whirling tasks on the daily merry-go-round still need to get done.

Plus, everything takes so much more effort when you're exhausted. Moving through the day is like trying to run underwater: it's twice as hard, but you're still stuck in slow motion. An office mate tells a joke, but it's ten minutes later before you finally get it and start laughing while sitting alone in your cube. And those morning meetings are perilous. You hope the boss doesn't turn the lights down for a power point presentation, for fear you'll break up the meeting with your snoring.

I know Jesus tells us we have to sacrifice for others: "Truly, truly, I say to you, unless a grain of wheat falls into the earth and dies, it remains alone; but if it dies, it bears much fruit. He who loves his life loses it, and he who hates his life in this world will keep it for eternal life." Jn 12, 24-25. I don't want to be alone. I'm glad that I have my wife and child, and I know I'm blessed.

But, couldn't I sacrifice something else? How about sports? I like watching sports, but I could give that up. I mean, I'm willing to sacrifice, if we can just agree on what the sacrifice ought to be. Is there any room for negotiation here?

How about money? I'll spring for the new stroller, or the fancy car seat. No problem.

But sleep . . .

I *really* like sleep.

I need it.

I don't want to give up my sleep.

I recently realized, while sitting in a rocking chair with a little bundle of joy in my arms and plenty of time to think between the hours of 1 a.m. and 2 a.m., that my attitude was more akin to that of the rich donors in the Bible story of the poor widow's sacrifice, Mk 12, 41-44, when as a father I'm called to be like the poor widow. Jesus watched in the temple as many rich people contributed large sums, and then He saw a poor widow who put in only two small coins worth a few cents. Jesus said: "Truly, I say to you, this poor widow has put in more than all those who are contributing to the treasury. For they all contributed out of their abundance; but she out of her poverty has put in everything she had, her whole living." Mk 12, 43-44.

That's the call of fatherhood. Raising kids takes more than just those things we don't mind parting with. Our kids need more than a few hours on the weekend, they need more than money. Our kids need *us*; all of us. Everything we can give them. Jesus told us: "Greater love has no man than this, that a man lay down his life for his friends." Jn, 15, 13. Jesus said: "If any man would come after me, let him deny himself and take up his cross and follow me." Mt 16, 24.

So let's learn a lesson from the poor widow, and the grain of wheat. To follow Jesus to eternal life, we've got to give fatherhood our all and give everything we have. After all, that's why the good Lord gave us double cappuccinos. Let's use them!

"Truth is not determined by a majority vote."

Cardinal Joseph Ratzinger (Pope Benedict XVI)

10.

Reality Check

My Dad and I were both working downtown and met for lunch one day. As we walked together a man stepped in front of us and asked for money.

I started to brush past him, but Dad stopped.

"I just got out of jail," the man said. "And I'm trying to get a job. But no one will hire me like this."

He was dirty, his clothes soiled, and he needed to shave and brush his teeth.

"But I've got a plan," he continued. "If I can get enough money for a hotel room, I can shower, wash my clothes in the sink, and then I can get a job."

Dad pulled out his wallet and gave the man a few bills.

"Thanks," the man said. "God bless you."

"You too," Dad answered, "and good luck."

We continued on our way, and I told Dad I never gave money to people on the street.

"I generally don't either," Dad said. "I don't like to encourage panhandling. But not all situations are the same. Remember that everything you have, and everything you are, is a gift to you from God. Whether you choose to give is up to you."

In the years since, I've often thought about that incident and stopped to remind myself that everything I have is given to me by God. As Jesus told the Twelve when commissioning them: "Without cost you have received; without cost you are to give." Mt 10, 10.

It's a reality check. A mental recalibration for times I sense my reasoning getting a little dodgy, like when I find myself thinking things like: *How can I be* really *sure how he'll use the money?* As a natural skinflint, I'm quite adept at deploying hypotheticals, theoreticals, and extrapolations of metaphysical possibilities projected into distant futurity to come up with reasons not to give. In *Why I'm Not a Pacifist*, C.S. Lewis said that such tendencies come from the corrupting influence of our passions on our reason. It's an occupational hazard of living: we human beings have a tremendous capacity for convincing ourselves that whatever we *want* is really what's right, after all.

Which is the deeper point embedded in Dad's observation. In living our faith, we have to use reason. As Scripture tells us:

> If you do good, know for whom you are doing it,
> and your kindness will have its effect. Do good to
> the just man and reward will be yours, if not from
> him, from the Lord. No good comes to him who
> gives comfort to the wicked, nor is it an act of
> mercy that he does. Give to the good man, refuse
> the sinner; refresh the downtrodden, give nothing to
> the proud man. No arms for combat should you give
> him, lest he use them against yourself; With twofold
> evil you will meet for every good deed you do for
> him. Sir 12, 1-6.

The brain must be engaged. We find truth not just in a torrent of emotion, or our own subjective feelings, but through the cooperation of our heart and head working together, along with plenty of prayer asking the Holy Spirit to guide the process.

And just as it's easy to fall into the 'Skeptic Septic'—the tendency of hyper-analysis for the ulterior purpose of riddling something with doubts, of stretching to find problems so that we'll have an excuse to avoid doing what we really don't want to do anyway—it's also easy to wind up in the 'No See Sewer.' That's when there really are problems present—but problems we'd rather not see, so we avert our eyes from the things we'd prefer not to notice and go ahead with what we want to do. Sometimes we just don't want to see the man behind the curtain, even if Toto is pulling on his pant leg. Like when the boss tells us to do what we think is wrong. Or when we want to go along with friends that we know are doing something we really shouldn't be involved in. Or when we want to join in what's billed as a feel-good cause and 'everyone is doing it.' We all want to be congenial, to be included, to be on the inside. (C. S. Lewis wrote a great reflection on this called *The Inner Ring*, which is included in the collection *The Weight of Glory*.) And sometimes even more than the desire to get along, we just want to avoid conflict and difficulty. (The manipulation of this strong desire so many feel to simply avoid conflict has propelled many a door-to-door salesman to riches.) No one wants to be the lone person called to stand against the crowd. We'd rather find some nice, anonymous place deep inside the herd where things feel much warmer and fuzzier and just plain safer.

But Scripture calls us to look; to see clearly; to know the good, and support it. Sir 12, 1-6. And Scripture tells us that we are not to do evil or support evil. Sir 12, 1-6.

So if we start to feel that niggling suspicion telling us our reasoning may be off-kilter, veering either toward the 'Skeptic Septic' or the 'No See Sewer,' it's time for a reality check. Jesus gave us a good one when He told us to remember that "whatever you did for one of these least brothers of mine, you did for me." Mt 26, 34, 40.

"What counts isn't how big the dog is in the fight, but how big the fight is in the dog."

Anonymous

11.

A Good Friday Devotion

When I was a kid my Mom used to embroider old sayings and decorate them with stitched designs and images. When she was done she'd frame them and hang them on the walls, so that walking through our house was a little tour through the patrimony of wisdom from the ages, all arrayed in a splendor of rainbow hues. I didn't give much thought to Mom's "Threads of Wisdom" at the time, but even without knowing it, I was absorbing those sayings into my bloodstream. Over the years I've been surprised at how they come unbidden to my mind at apropos moments, complete with visions of needlework patterns and pictures. A favorite of Mom's was: "There are only two lasting bequests we can give our children, roots and wings."

One of the roots Mom and Dad cultivated for us kids was a simple Good Friday devotion. It was this: from noon to 3 p.m. on Good Friday we were not to eat, drink, or talk. Each of us children, and Mom and Dad also, were to go somewhere by ourselves and contemplate the Passion of Jesus Christ. We could take a Bible with us to read the Passion narrative if we wished (which I usually did). We could also take a Rosary and pray the sorrowful mysteries (which I usually did also).

I still remember those quiet afternoons of solitude and reflection. We each had our own special place where we usually spent our Good Friday observance. One of my brothers took the platform on the garage roof that Dad built to serve as our astronomical observatory. A sister took the scaffolding "tree house": a section of left-over scaffolding Dad had made for some home repairs. When he finished the work on the house, he set up a section of the scaffolding under a tree in the backyard as a fort for us kids. It was just the right height to get you up in the branches with a leafy green canopy for a roof.

My spot was on an old car Dad had salvaged and kept parked out back by the garage, just off the alley. I would sit on the hood of the car and use the windshield for a back rest as I read the Passion and prayed the Rosary and watched the clouds while thinking about the sacrifice of Jesus Christ.

Years later, after college and law school, I fell out of regular church attendance. Not that I ever made a conscious decision to quit going to church. It was just that starting my career I worked long hours, with lots of nights and weekends, and very little free time outside of work. When I wasn't in the office, I was usually exhausted and I'd just crash. I'd order a huge slab of ribs, maybe a pizza or two, and gorge myself like a lion on the Serengeti bellying up to a fresh, steaming Wildebeest. Then, just like that lion after his big feed, I'd take my distended belly off to a nice, quiet place for a long sleep. Upon resurfacing into the world of consciousness, it was usually time to get the dry-cleaning, shine my shoes, and start it all over again.

And somewhere in that hectic cycle of work, dry-cleaning and shoe-shining, a lot of other things fell by the wayside, left behind like a bag of groceries forgotten at the check-out line. Too many distractions: cell phones ringing, errands to run, and already late for the next appointment. Life was busy, there was lots of noise, and somehow while my attention was diverted elsewhere, things slipped through the cracks. But then in the midst of the mayhem, Good Friday would come along, and that old family devotion always managed to cut through the clamor of the world.

Usually it came to me as I was shaving in the morning. I'd start think about the Easter weekend coming up, remember it was Good Friday, and then recall afternoons sitting on that car. As I'd rush to get dressed and knot my tie, I had a spate of reasons why it wouldn't be a good idea to keep the old family devotion *this* year—chief among them the fasting, and the fact that I never ate breakfast before work, and I always looked ravenously forward to lunch—though I always manfully resolved that I would start keeping the devotion again. Next year.

But then as I had a little quiet time sitting alone in the car driving to work, I always knew I had to do it. I'd vow to remember

49

Good Friday earlier next year, so that I could plan ahead and eat breakfast before work, but I'd keep the Good Friday devotion *today*, imperfect as my preparations and readiness may be. And so, come noon, for three hours, rusty as I might be at spending time with God, I would fast and be silent and pray, and try to meditate on the Passion of Christ. (And not cheeseburgers.)

Now, I realize that three hours of fasting isn't going to put you in the ascetic hall of fame, but some is better than none. Like G. K. Chesterton said, "If a thing is worth doing, it is worth doing badly." Besides, compared to the zero hours dedicated over the rest of the twelve months, Good Friday represented a 300% increase for the year. What really mattered was that the little devotion started by Mom and Dad had the power to reach out to me decades later and bring me back to something I hadn't even realized I'd forgotten.

The Catechism of the Catholic Church recognizes the importance of homespun devotions:

> At its core the piety of the people is a storehouse of values that offers answers of Christian wisdom to the great questions of life. The Catholic wisdom of the people is capable of fashioning a vital synthesis . . . It creatively combines the divine and the human, Christ and Mary, spirit and body, communion and institution, person and community, faith and homeland, intelligence and emotion. This wisdom is a Christian humanism that radically affirms the dignity of every person as a child of God, establishes a basic fraternity, teaches people to encounter nature and understand work, provides reasons for joy and humor even in the midst of a very hard life. CCC 1676

Traditions of the domestic church are bearers of the faith to the next generation. As Hilaire Belloc put it: "Now the Faith is not taught. It is inhabited and breathed in." (*The Essential Belloc*, edited by McCloskey, Bloch, Robertson.) The faith is more lived than learned, more caught than taught, and it's from our family—

those with whom we inhabit and breathe—that it's most often caught.

Family devotions are a big part of that. Easter hams, candlelit evening Rosaries, religious pictures, reading out loud, crafts, statues of the saints, and seasonal carols, all play their part in conveying different aspects of the great Faith that's been gifted to us. The very tangibility of feasting and fasting, song and silence, light and dark, help the roots take hold. Smells and bells are important. In his book *As I Lay Dying*, Father Richard John Neuhaus said that we humans have "tactile" memory, embodied beings that we are, so that "even [our] thinking is sensuous. . . [our] recollections touching the burlap of disappointments and . . . the velvet of joys recalled."

Father Barron wrote in *Catholicism*, the companion book to his movie series:

> In the ancient world when a young man joined a philosophical school, say Plato's academy, he was not simply enrolling in a series of classes or course of lectures in Platonic philosophy. He was signing on for an entire style of life, involving practices and bodily disciplines, as well as new patterns of thought. We find something very similar in the Acts of the Apostles, where the early Christian church is referred to as "the Way," a term that catches this practical, embodied dimension of Catholic life.

A family is vastly more powerful than any philosophical school. Thus C. S. Lewis wrote in *The Abolition of Man*, "I had sooner play cards against a man who was quite skeptical about ethics, but bred to believe that 'a gentleman does not cheat', than against an irreproachable moral philosopher who had been brought up among sharpers." And each family is its own "Way," in that each family has its own practical, embodied life which is teaching all the time, whether we will it or no—and perhaps more so at the times we aren't conscious of teaching than at the times of intentional disquisition.

We all want to do something to change the world, especially these days. The good news is that we don't have to launch a new philosophical movement to do it. Something far more powerful and effective has already been entrusted into our hands: our families. For those of us with children, we are changing the world every day in our role as parents. And even if we don't have kids, we are sons and daughters, brothers and sisters, aunts and uncles, spiritual mothers and fathers, and a helping hand for those in need—and it's all in the family, since we all have the same Father. To change the world, we don't have to look any further than the dining room table. It was John Paul the Great said: "As the family goes, so the nation and so goes the whole world in which we live."

Now that's a saying worthy of Mom's needles and thread.

"It is a good idea sometimes to think of the importance and dignity of our every-day duties. It keeps them from being so tiresome; besides, others are apt take us at our own valuation."

Laura Ingalls Wilder

12.

Easter

A few days before Easter our clan would gather around the dining room table, cover it with newspapers, and get dirty. Or rather: colorful. Lots of little fingers got stained purple, pink and green while dipping hard boiled eggs into cups of dye. The more artistically inclined among us would draw crayon designs on their eggs, and the more patient would create multi-colored eggs by balancing an egg on a spoon in one pot of dye so that only half the egg was submerged, waiting until that color took hold, and then balancing the same egg on another spoon in another cup of dye so that the other half was dyed a different color (usually with a third bonus color in a band where the other two met in the middle). The air smelled of the vinegar Mom and Dad used to juice up the potency of the dyes—and the house was full of laughter from the joy and jocularity Mom and Dad used to juice up the whole event. At the end of the evening we'd have a basket filled with a rainbow hued array of ovoid artistic creations—and hearts full of memories. And the memories were the real masterpieces.

When Easter itself finally rolled around, we started out the morning with a dash outside in our PJ's looking for another Easter egg: this one drawn in chalk on the sidewalk in front of our house (or on the porch if rain threatened). It was a very special egg, reputed to have been rendered by the very paws of the Easter Bunny himself (which we knew to be Mom and Dad, knowledge that diminished the fun of it not one whit). The chalk drawing was always an egg worthy of Faberge, done in multiple colors, with all manner of cross-hatching, swirls and designs. But the most important thing to us kids wasn't the artistic finery: it was the number in the middle of the egg. That number was, according to family lore, The Mark of the Easter Bunny, drawn to show how many Easter baskets the Bunny had hidden inside the house. Fortunately, we always had a 100% correspondence between the number in the chalk egg and the number of children residing on the premises.

Once we had seen the chalk egg, we had to hurry to get ready for church. We were not allowed to search for our hidden Easter baskets—or eat any candy—until after mass (Mom and Dad were wily that way). Not that the prohibition on searching precluded all indulgences of curiosity. There is a lot of snooping that can be done without crossing the line into what technically constitutes "searching," as that term is used in the industry. After all, we kids had to get scrubbed and brushed and resplendent in our dapper new Easter duds, and you can do a lot of moseying around the house while dressing and tending to the requirements of personal hygiene. Hey, the living room is just as good a place to brush your teeth as the bathroom (at least on Easter Sunday it is). And while you're enjoying a fresh minty toothpaste perambulation, why not take a little look-see behind the big curtains on the front windows? That's not searching. It's just enjoying the view of the wall behind the curtains—you usually don't get to see that particular patch of wall nearly enough, you know. Oh, and come to think of it, I wonder if I left my shoes inside the kitchen hutch last night? You never can tell. Better check just to be sure.

There was plenty of whispering among the ranks as all this meandering church preparation went on. By surreptitiously sharing information back and forth, between the lot of us we were usually able to identify the hidden locations of all the baskets before the last clip-on tie was put in place and it was time to go. And when we were finally all ready, gussied up and decked out in our new Easter threads (Easter always meant new dresses for the girls and new suits for the boys), we headed out to the front steps for the annual Easter photo.

Every year we'd take a picture on the steps in front of our house before going to mass, and it's funny to see all those pictures together now. It's almost like a stop-action, time-lapse animation: all those kids growing taller and taller year after year in picture after picture, right before your eyes. It's also a good chance to compare changing fashion trends over the past several decades. After careful consideration, I gotta say the Eighties represent the apogee of American style—Magnum PI will always be the King of Cool in my book (not that I'm dating myself or anything).

With the yearly photo complete, we loaded into the van and headed for church. For us kids the highlight of the Easter mass was at the very end, when the priest caterwauled The Great Alleluia. Especially when it was Father Coughlin. He was about 99 years old and thin as a post. The rest of the year he was quiet and almost frail seeming. But come Easter Sunday, stand back! He was a veritable force of nature when he let a Great Alleluia rip—the rafters shook and you *knew* you were listening to a True Believer.

When we got home after mass, still tingling in our toes from the aftershocks of Father's Great Alleluia, it was finally time to get those Easter baskets. While us kids scurried about retrieving baskets and commenced the unwrapping of Easter surprises, Mom laid out the feast: a giant ham dripping glaze and covered with pineapples and cloves, Polish sausage, baked beans with bacon, olives, punch with floating icebergs of sherbet, homemade potato salad, Hawaiian bread, and all the other trimmings. I always loved the real food of that feast more than the Easter candy—especially Mom's homemade potato salad. Not that my chocolate bunny was neglected. It was usually de-eared before Mom was done lading the table. But as soon as the food line was open, the earless bunny went back in the basket and I hustled to grab a spot in the queue for deliciousness, eager to pile my plate. But high as I'd pile it, it wasn't long before I was back in line again for seconds, and then thirds—it was a hobbit kind of feast: firsts, seconds, thirdsies, in-betweens, etc. And best of all, back in those days I didn't swoon into a semi-comatose state and head for the couch after that kind of feed. Instead, I went out to play!

As festivities moved outdoors it was time to blow bubbles and launch rockets. Every year we got a collection of Nerf balls, balsa wood gliders, and little red plastic rockets in our Easter baskets. The rockets came with an air pump, and you filled the rocket part way with water, then pumped air into it until the pump couldn't force anymore air in. With the rocket primed, you moved out to an open space in the yard with no trees overhead, released the lever, and *Whoosh*! The rocket tore off into the sky like a NASA moon launch, leaving a trail of foaming water streaking through the air behind it. It was thrilling for a 9 year old (and who am I kidding, I still love those things!).

55

So passed our Easter: running, launching rockets, blowing bubbles, throwing Nerf balls, and gliding gliders, with periodic breaks to go back inside for more feast, then heading back outside for more play. Spring was in the air, the grass was green, trees were fuzzy with a million little buds of new leaves, and the family was all together.

It was a wonderful day of exuberant living—which is really what Easter is all about. As Scott Hahn explained in *Did Not Our Hearts Burn Within Us*, his lecture series on the Gospel of Luke, "in the Catholic tradition, we recognize that salvation is not just *from* sin, salvation is *for* sharing divine life," so that we can be "filled with the fullness of Trinitarian life, which is the ultimate goal of salvation." (Emphasis added.)

Jesus said: "I came so that they might have life and have it more abundantly." Jn 10, 10. And, as Father Robert Barron put it, Easter is our "Victory Day," the day Christ won that new life for us—life in abundance. No wonder Easter brought out Father Coughlin's electrifying Alleluia. It's a day for all creatures great and small to thank God and shout out to the heavens: Alleluia!

Finally, brethren,
whatever is true,
whatever is honorable,
whatever is just,
whatever is pure,
whatever is lovely,
whatever is gracious,
if there is any excellence,
if there is anything worthy of praise,
think about these things.

Saint Paul, Philippians 4, 8.

13.

Give Me a Call

It's probably hard to imagine now, but the world did exist before e-mail. And even, if you can believe it, before cell phones.

I know, it sounds crazy. But it's true. I was there and I can tell you about it.

In those halcyon days, no one uttered the words "internet" or "mobile communication network." "Can you hear me now?" was something you said from the next room, not the other side of the country.

I started my first job and moved to a new city for the first time in this archaic period of joyful disconnection, when a person could be blissfully unable to be reached everywhere, all the time.

To keep in touch with family and friends you didn't blog, post, tweet or send mass e-mails.

You used the Pony Express.

OK, I'm just kidding about that. But really, to keep in touch you either put pen to paper and wrote a real letter—we're talking ink on pressed tree pulp—or you made a telephone call. When we made telephone calls, we didn't even know we were using a "land line." They were just phones, and they were all connected to wires, whether it was your home phone or a pay phone—a contraption that has all but disappeared. It's still strange to me that you don't see pay phones around like you used to. It was 25 cents to place a local call on the venerable old pay phone. Long distance was expensive, whether you were using a pay phone or your home phone, and you tried not to talk too long. Stamps, on the other hand, were only 18 cents.

Since I had seven siblings, I opted for the lower priced United States Postal Service as my preferred method of communication. Plus, I like writing letters.

But I learned that not everyone shares that enthusiasm: I mailed out many letters, but got few in return. One of my brothers,

Mark, was particularly recalcitrant. From the other siblings I'd at least get an occasional note. It was never a one-for-one reply for every letter I sent, but there was enough correspondence to let me know my letters weren't being misdirected to Siberia.

Except for Mark. I *never* got a letter from him. Not even one. If Mom didn't assure me that he still showed-up at the house on days when she made perogis, I'd have thought Mark had been misdirected to Siberia. But since he turned up when the food was cooking, I figured he was getting my letters, and just wasn't writing back.

So I wrote him more letters. I showered him with correspondence like I was running a mail order catalogue business with a target market of only one: Mark—all in an attempt to embarrass him into replying by the sheer quantity of pages I sent. To no effect. Still no letter came in reply. So I began cajoling Mark in my many missives to send me some kind of response. Cajoling also failed to produce results.

So I finally took a drastic step. I sent him a self-addressed, stamped envelope with instructions on how to use the United States Postal Service. I explained the wonders of the mail: Mark merely needed to place a letter in the envelope and deposit the envelope in a post-box. The vast machinery of the US Federal government would then grind into operation. Legions of blue clad US Postal Service employees would pass that letter from hand to hand and truck to truck all across the country until at last it was finally delivered right to my door. All for just 18 cents. An amazing service. The best bargain in town. I encouraged Mark to take advantage of this stupendous deal and send me a letter.

Then, one day when I got home from work, I was shocked. Awaiting me in the mail box was the self-addressed, stamped envelope I had sent to Mark! I tore it open. Inside was one page. Taped to that one page was a quarter. There was a one line note written on the page: "If you want to talk to me, use this to give me a call sometime."

Mark.

He was an ornery one. Still is. And I still have that letter.

But Mark finally helped me realize, way back then, that you need to let people be who they are. No matter how right we may consider our ways of doing things, trying to force others to conform to *us* isn't a good thing. Sometimes we need to meet people where they are.

I thought of Mark's quarter when I read something that God told us in the Bible about our kids (and really about ourselves). God said: "Before I formed you in the womb I knew you . . ." Jer 1, 5.

It was God who formed each of us in the womb, "the Lord, Who created you . . . and formed you . . ." Is 43, 1. And it was God who created our kids: "Thus says the Lord, your redeemer, Who formed you from the womb: I am the Lord, Who made all things . . ." Is 44, 24. Isaiah puts it beautifully: ". . . O Lord, You are our father; we are the clay and You the potter: we are all the work of Your hands." Is 64, 3.

God made each of us, and He made us the way *He* wanted us to be: "I formed you to be a servant to me . . ." Is 44, 21. "Everyone . . . whom I created for My glory, whom I formed and made . . ." Is 43, 7. ". . . the Lord called me from birth, from my mother's womb He gave me my name." Is 49, 1. ". . . the Lord has spoken Who formed me as His servant from the womb . . ." Is 49, 5.

We need to respect that. We might not understand why more people don't see things the way we do, or why more people aren't like us—especially when it's our own kids. But then, God Himself told us: "You question me about my children, or prescribe the work of my hands for me! It was I who made the earth and created mankind upon it; It was my hands that stretched out the heavens . . ." Is 45, 11-12.

Sometimes it's just good to be reminded of how things really are. And the humility we need to cultivate in the face of God's design extends to our kids. It can be frustrating when our kids don't do what we want them to, whether it's the toddler who refuses to cooperate for his naps or the adult child who takes that job in a distant city we wish they'd turn down. But we have to remember to respect our kids as the children of God that they are, made as God intended them to be, and let them do the work that God created them to do.

We might want them to write letters, but they may be telephone people.

Which may just turn out for the best, anyway. Nowadays long distance calls are free and it costs 43 cents to mail a letter. Who would have predicted that 10 years ago? We can't see how all the parts of life and the world work together even now, at this very moment, let alone anticipate how things will look in the future.

We can't, but God can.

Even when we don't understand it, even when we don't *like* it, we have to trust in Him and let all the works of His hands do what they were created to do.

"Life is what we make it, always has been, always will be."

Grandma Moses

14

Bread and Fire

There is beauty in the world. There is peace in the world. There is joy. In fact, there's lots of it. Only, there's lots of other stuff too. Sometimes trying to recognize the good things is like trying to find the right web-site. Your search returns 6 million hits. So where's the one you want? It's there somewhere, but buried within 5 million nine-hundred-ninety-nine thousand nine-hundred-ninety-nine distractions. Each one a little dust mote floating in the sunshine of life. And as anyone who's driven across country can attest, as the miles pile up those dust motes have a way of accumulating into a dark, muddy smear.

Still, despite the millions of specks of road grit spackled to the windshield (along with who knows what else), the beauty is still out there—even when you can't see it. And sometimes, when we're having a particularly difficult time recognizing it, it will even find us—sneaking up to spring on us unawares like a lion. As it did for me last night.

Our eight month old daughter woke sometime deep in the dark of night. I stumbled bleary-eyed and groggy to her crib. When you're that tired, I don't even know how you function. Maybe Mr. Miyagi was right in *The Karate Kid* when he told Ralph Macchio: "Wax on, wax off"—endless repetition may actually ingrain certain motions so deeply in the muscle fiber that they become automatic. Only for parents it's not karate moves, its stupendous feats of hygiene daring, as in: "Diaper on, diaper off."

Anyway, somehow I managed to get her diaper changed and make a bottle while on auto-pilot, all the while aided by the sweet strains of nocturnal wailing from a little baby that sounded the way I felt: desperate to get back to sleep.

I was beginning to emerge from semi-consciousness as I weaved a weary way to the rocking chair by the picture window in our living room, one hand holding the baby, now swathed in clean britches fresh as a spring breeze, the other hand clutching optimistically to the warm bottle I was counting-on to lull my progeny back to the somnolence I hoped to regain shortly for my own self as well.

I sat down and for a few minutes there was intent and vigorous sucking as our daughter powered down six ounces of creamy formula-bliss. Then in a dramatic moment, she released the nipple from the vice-grip of her toothless gums and pushed the bottle away. I waited with my breath held. Was she about to wail . . . or sail, sweetly back to the realm of dreams?

She wriggled, she wiggled, then snuggled up against me. There was a contented sigh . . . and suddenly she was back to sleepy land.

"*Ahhh*," I sighed, too.

I looked down at her lovely little face nestled in the crook of my arm. Her eyes closed, a smile dimpling her chubby apple-dumpling cheeks, an expression of contentment and serenity across her brow, with "moonlight flowing over all" from the open window. (Longfellow.)

It was beautiful.

I was surprised by a moment of joy.

It wasn't the frothy kind of jocularity that goes with party-hats and off-key singing, but the quiet, seeping all the way down into your bones kind of joy that's almost too much to bear. The kind of joy that makes you believe in Heaven. As George Weigel said in *Letters to a Young Catholic*, it was the kind of "beauty [that] helps prepare us to be . . . . people who can be comfortable in heaven—the kind of people who can live with God forever."

Scripture tells us: "The earth, though out of it comes forth bread, is in fiery upheaval underneath." Job 28, 5.

We're all familiar with the fiery upheaval. Not just sleepless nights or crying babies, but real trials, pain, and heartache. Ugliness, loss, regrets, wounds—wounds that don't seem to heal, or at least that will take longer to heal than they've had so far. The fiery upheaval is real too, and it hurts.

Yet, amidst the upheavals, the joy is there, and it's also real.

Maybe when we find ourselves ambushed unexpectedly by joy and beauty it's because God has sent them out on a search-and-

62

rescue mission to track us down and remind us that good things are still out there.

And to give us our own marching orders: go forth and find them yourself.

And even more than just finding them (difficult as that can be sometimes): *grow them*. For yourself, and for others.

Though in emergencies God may send forth the Lion of Joy and Beauty to stalk us down and drag us with its powerful jaws back into the light, we really can't wait for joy and beauty to sneak-up on us, any more than we'd wait for a chance rainstorm to clean our windshield on a cross-country road-trip. While we're driving we use the wiper-blades and an automated squirt of washer-fluid to fight the build-up of grime as we go along, and when we get a chance to stop at a gas station it's time to deploy the big squeegee-brush to get the windows clean all the way to the edges, where the wiper-blades don't reach. We keep on cleaning the windows throughout the journey, both so we can enjoy the magnificent scenery, and to be sure we don't wind-up in a ditch on the side of the road.

Beauty and joy need some proactive participation on our part, too. We can seek them out, sustain them where we find them, and nurture them—along with nurturing our own capacity and appreciation for them. It's part of our calling as Christians, especially those of us who are parents. Because it's not just we big people who need them. Our children also need beauty and joy, like flowers need the rain, to help them grow and blossom into the people of beauty and joy prepared for Heaven that God intends them to be.

It's a life-long quest, but we don't make the journey alone. God is with us every step of the way, through the fiery upheaval as well as in the times of beauty and joy. Enduring the fires, we pray. In the moments of joy, we thank God for the bread that sustains us!

15.

Collision with the Dentyne Truck

Imagine the scene: A businessman strides briskly through an airport. Coming upon one of those airport convenience stores with piratical prices, he stops, turns inside, and purchases a dozen packs of Dentyne gum.

Then he walks back out into the bustle of the airport and finds an out-of-the-way spot next to a big, leafy, fake plant where he can avoid the rush of people hurrying to their gates. There he sets down his brief case and commences opening pack after pack of Dentyne gum. With each pack he opens, he takes out every stick of gum it contains and tucks pieces of Dentyne into the pockets of his coat and shirt. When those are full, sticks of gum go into the knot of his tie, inside the collar of his shirt, up his sleeves and into his shoes and socks. He even hides little sticks of Dentyne in his mop of curly hair. Sticks of Dentyne have even been known to lodge behind his ears.

As the businessman continues secreting Dentyne about his person, he attracts the attention of rubber-neckers craning to watch him even as they hustle to their flights. *What the heck is that guy doing?*

When the last piece of gum is hidden, the now Dentyne-laden businessman picks up his briefcase again and heads out to hail a cab.

And now, as Paul Harvey would say, for the rest of the story: we see the cab from the airport pull-up outside a small, unremarkable brown house on a very average and forgettable street in a small town, somewhere deep in "fly-over America," that never makes the news and that most people have never heard of. As the businessman leans forward to pay his fare, a stray piece of Dentyne falls onto the seat next to the cabbie. While the businessman collects his errant stick of gum and hands the cabbie money, little faces begin appearing at the windows of the small brown house.

When the businessman finally steps out of the taxi, a shout of "Daddy!" goes up as eight young voices join in a chorus yelling the magic name.

"Daddy is home!"

They're so loud you can hear them outside, their excited, high pitched yelling practically rattling the windowpanes.

No matter how the trip went, whether sales were high or only expenses (and when it's your own business you feel every penny of expenses), the businessman breaks into a smile and bounds up the stairs to throw open the front door. When he does, he's mobbed by little arms grabbing him from all sides.

Finally one of the children will look up with wide eyes and ask, "Did you see the Dentyne truck, Daddy?"

"Why yes," Dad answers. "The Dentyne truck had an accident on the road just as my taxi was going past and gum was flying everywhere!"

"Yeah!" everyone cheers.

Somehow Daddy always has the good fortune to drive through a cloud of gum on his way home from the airport.

All the kids set-to, searching for hidden Dentyne, and by long experience they know to look in Daddy's hair and shoes and inside the collar of his shirt. The search goes on with plenty of laughter and the kids telling Daddy about school and baseball games, and Daddy sharing stories of the far-away places he's visited, exotic locals like Rapid City, Iowa and Jasper, Indiana.

The businessman was my Dad, and how he ever got the idea of dousing himself in Dentyne I don't know, but it was a stroke of genius us kids loved. Dentyne is still my favorite gum.

Dad may have endured a lot of funny looks in airports, but as our Heavenly Father told us in Scripture: "My thoughts are not your thoughts, nor are your ways My ways . . ." Is 55, 8. And so it is with our earthly fathers: the ways and thoughts of a parent are not the same as those without children.

I've learned this myself since having kids. Now it seems perfectly natural to me to stroll through a store singing, "Doe, a deer, a female deer," so that our older daughter can belt out her favorite line, "Ray! A drop of Golden Sun!" from the basket of the grocery cart. I get my own share of raised eyebrows. But then, I also collect a fair number of smiles. I know from which reaction I get who's versed in the wily ways of kids and who remains uninitiated.

After church one Sunday, I was shaking hands with our pastor as we filed out and he stopped me and said, "I saw you dancing in the pew like a crazy man," referring to my swaying back-and-forth with one of our daughters to try to keep her happy in the waning moments of a long mass. "But it was a beautiful dance," our pastor continued. "It's the dance of love."

That's the vocation of parenting. It's an invitation to join in the dance of love, a call to experience the jolt of a radical love that can be as crazy as a collision with a Dentyne truck. It can certainly be jarring at times, but our pastor was right: it is beautiful. So jump in! Sing and dance, use your imagination—and let the Lord lead!

". . . first you make your habits, and then your habits make you . . . word to the wise: if you want to improve your life, improve your habits."

From *Hugs, Daily Inspiration for Women*

16.

A Gift

My sister Agnes is a hoot. Whip-smart, fast with the one-liners, and full of fun. I love talking to her on the phone. Calls from Agnes are events. I get a drink, kick-back on the couch, and prepare to laugh.

She always calls me from the road when she's driving home to Mom & Dad's house. I'm 6 hours and one state closer to the homestead than Agnes, so when the clan is all gathering I usually get there before she does. One of the states Agnes has to traverse to reach kith and kin is Wisconsin (or Wisco as Agnes calls it). Agnes isn't just fast with the one-liners, she also knows how to motor when she wants to lay down tracks. And she always seems to get a lot of tickets in Wisco.

In fact, the tickets, Agnes explained to me, are what prompt her Formula-One approach to the Dairy State.

"That's why I drive so fast in Wisco," Agnes said. "I try to get through before they give me another ticket."

Once when all hands were gathering back at the old homestead, Agnes called me when I was already home. Mom heard me talking to her on my cell phone and said: "Ask Agnes if she wants me to get something ready for her to eat when she gets here."

I asked Agnes.

"No," Agnes answered, "I don't eat anything at Mom and Dad's house until I check the expiration dates in the fridge first."

I dutifully reported Agnes' retort to the gathered assembly, and it met with much merriment and guffawing.

But not one to be outdone, Mom took a black marker, went into the fridge, and crossed-out all the expiration dates on every bottle, jug and jar in the whole thing. When Agnes got there, she went to the fridge to find a snack, and we all knew when she'd

67

found Mom's little surprise, because Agnes has one of those big laughs that fills a house and gets everyone else laughing too.

Little zany things like that always seem to spring up when Agnes is around.

She's also solid in a pinch. If you already spent that bonus check that was promised, then discover it isn't coming through after all, you can count on Agnes.

I won't go into all the stories. I can't. Most of them I don't know. That's because Agnes never says anything when she helps someone out. Some people, if they put 50 cents in the bell-ringer's bucket at Christmas, you'll still be hearing about it come Easter. Which isn't always (or ever) so great. Sometimes if you're in a bit of a jam, it can hurt to have details of your predicament broadcast far and wide. That's usually even tougher than the original problem itself.

Well, with Agnes, you don't have to worry. If Agnes gives someone the coat off her back, the only way you'll know about it is if you see her shivering in the cold—and she's pretty tough. She doesn't shiver easy.

Agnes is the Double-O-Seven of good works. Licensed to *Good Will*. She's a secret agent of kindness, the stealth fighter of corporal works of mercy. Jokes and stories a-plenty she'll share, but never a piece of gossip.

Agnes isn't just a sister, she's a blessing, one of the people about whom Scripture says: "Barter not a friend for money, nor a dear brother for . . . gold . . ." Sir 7, 18. "A faithful friend is a sturdy shelter, he who finds one finds a treasure. A faithful friend is beyond price, no sum can balance his worth. A faithful friend is a lifesaving remedy . . ." Sir 6, 14-16. "Two are better than one . . . If the one falls, the other will lift up his companion." Eccl 4, 9-10. "[A] brother is born for the time of stress." Prv 17, 17.

Brothers and sisters are a tremendous gift to our children— far better than any material thing. It surprises me when people say it's bad to have lots of kids. They say a kid should have his own room, piles of new clothes, a car at 16, and college paid for by their parents. But Scripture has a different value system. The Bible tells us that none of these things compare to a brother or sister. Who would choose a shirt over a human life? Better to have a brother to share your room, than a room alone. And long after a car is rusting in some junk yard, siblings will still have each other. As for college, a sister rooting for you to get that scholarship is a lot more fun than being alone when you come home from school for the holidays. If a kid needs to go to a less expensive college, or take out a loan, that's alright—his family will be with him on graduation day and long after any loan's paid off.

So instead of a car, give your kids a family. Joy. Memories. Nights of laughing and swapping stories into the wee hours, rather than sitting alone in front of a fancy entertainment center. A helping hand through thick-and-thin their whole life. We won't be around for our kids their whole life, but after we're gone their brothers and sisters will still be there for each other: helping, laughing, loving. That's what life is really about.

A man asked Jesus, "Where were you when I needed you?" Jesus answered, "Look back on your life." The man looked back, and saw footprints in the sand. Jesus said: "Where you see two sets of footprints, that is where I walked beside you. Where you see one set of footprints, that is where I carried you. Where you see the two grooves in the sand, that's where I dragged you kicking and screaming."

Anonymous

17.

What We've Got

Sometimes I marvel at the creative power of the human mind. Like whoever first thought of grabbing wind out of the sky and putting it to work for us. Someone, somewhere long ago, needed more grain milled. What to do? Get more serfs, hire more hands, harness more horses. But what if you don't have serfs or money or horses? "Well," the unknown but audacious innovator thought, "the wind is free for the taking. I'll use that." Propeller-powered electric-turbines and the TVA weren't far behind.

I had a similar eureka moment, albeit on a much smaller, more prosaic scale, with our eighteen month old daughter. Liz was helping me make veggie soup, and you know how little helpers can slow the process down. First she stood on her stool at the sink and we washed carrots together (each clean carrot yielding about a gallon of water on the kitchen floor). Next we moved her stool over to the chopping station. There an elaborate ritual developed for getting carrots from the cutting board into the soup. Daddy cut a piece of carrot, then placed the piece on the counter in front of Liz so she could "dump" it in the pot. Every time I delivered a piece of carrot, Liz said "Thank you." I said, "You're welcome," and then she took the little carrot nubbin in her hand, declared: "Dump!" and dropped the nubbin into the pot. With one piece successfully added to the soup, it was time to repeat the entire process with another tiny little chunk of carrot—every step observed with the care of a ceremonial tea from the ancient Orient.

The only thing with ceremonial teas from Medieval Asia is: they take a lot of time. So I started singing to help while away the idle moments between my produce handling duties, selecting a classic from the oeuvre of timeless vocal-music: "The ABC Song," to be precise. Liz bopped her head and danced along to the lilting strains of "A-B-C . . ." as we slowly filled our pot. But despite its status as a lyrical masterwork, we had five carrots to work our way through, and Daddy began to tire of the alphabet song after 10 or 15 renditions.

I stopped singing and said, "Well, let's see now, what next."

"Music," Liz said.

"You want music?" I asked.

"Again," Liz answered.

"Again?" I asked, "should I put a CD on?"

"No," Liz said. "ABC."

Queen Elizabeth had spoken. Daddy took a deep breath, cleared his throat, and began once more: "A, B, C, D, E, F, G . . ."

Liz smiled and went back to be-bopping on her stool. "Dump!" she declared, and another piece of carrot plopped into the pot.

I smiled, too. First to have my singing called "music." But second, at the realization that a smile and a happy afternoon for our daughter was free for the asking. It didn't take dolls whose clothes cost more than mine, or play-structures you needed a building permit to erect. A little joy for Liz was as free as a song.

Sometimes we parents fall into the trap of worrying about all the things we can't give our children—from toys when they're little to cars and college tuition when they're bigger. We forget that you make a life out of what you have, not what you lack, and overlook the things right under our noses that we can use to create a good life for our kids and ourselves right now—like playhouses made from cardboard boxes, or a song and a pile of carrots and a pot for soup.

In the Acts of the Apostles, as Peter and John went into the temple one day, a crippled beggar asked them for alms. Peter answered: "I have neither silver nor gold, but what I do have I give you: in the name of Jesus Christ the Nazorean, rise and walk." Peter took the man by his hand and raised him up, and the man was cured and walked into the temple with them. Acts 3, 6-8.

That's what we can do as parents: give what we have. And sometimes we are all like the crippled beggar, outside the temple looking to gold and silver and things of this world for our cure. But the things that can heal us, the things that really matter, are from God. Things like truth, faith, joy, courage, peace. The things that can't be bought. Instead of focusing on what we don't have, if we take stock of the gifts already given us, and the things available to us without a price tag, we may be surprised at the resources we can draw upon, and all that we can do with them. Like the audacious innovator who first grabbed wind out of the sky, we can take hold of the graces offered us to transform our world, starting with our own families. Then we too may be healed, rise, and enter into the temple.

"Be kind, for everyone you meet is fighting a hard battle."

Plato

18.

Negotiating with God

My Dad was in on the ground floor of computing, back when they were still laying the floors. He used to take us to his office when he'd work weekends, so even though I'm only marginally computer-literate myself, I remember all kinds of old, wonky computer-geek stuff. Like stacks of "punch cards"— cardboard tickets with little rectangular holes punched in them. The holes somehow constituted the 'code' that ran the computers. Those little hole-punched cards were the first transferable 'storage media.' And I remember the first 'portable' computers. Dad brought one home one day, in a padded bag the size of a suitcase. It weighed about 40 pounds—and probably had less computing power than the average cell phone does today.

But those old machines were cutting edge in their time, and those early days were heady for everyone involved in the emerging new technology. The whole field of computers was wide open and still being shaped. There were no Microsofts or Apples, at least not as the massive market hegemonies they've become. Back then Bill Gates and Steve Jobs were working out of their garages just like everyone else. It was the Klondike days of computing. One person with inspiration and the grit to see it through to realization could skyrocket from the garage to riches. It didn't require pools of capital or board room conglomerates to get off the ground. Just ideas and guts. And maybe a little bit of luck.

My Dad knew a few who made it big. One of those who soared it into the stratosphere told Dad about his big break. The guy had written a new computer program, and he had an interested buyer. The buyer was flying through, with a lay-over of a few hours at a nearby airport, so they arranged to meet at the airport.

Dad's friend drove to the airport and found the potential buyer at his gate. They shook hands, then retired to an airport bar to talk turkey.

"I can't pay more than two," the buyer said, opening negotiations.

The programmer had hoped for more, but remember this was 3 or 4 decades ago, when the median annual income for a family was about $6,000.

"I couldn't let it go for less than five," the programmer responded.

They haggled from there, with the programmer giving ground, until they finally settled on three.

"Alright," the programmer agreed, "three it is."

The buyer had a form contract in his briefcase. He took it out, filled in the numbers, signed it, and pushed it across the table to the programmer. The programmer scanned the contract, took the pen proffered by the buyer, and signed his name.

"Good doing business with you," the buyer said, collecting his contract. "I hate to run, but I've got another flight to catch."

The programmer shook his hand. "Good doing business with you, too."

The buyer left, but the programmer remained. As he told my Dad later: "I sat there for hours. I was stunned. When I looked at the contract . . . I'd been talking thousands, but he was talking millions."

I think of that story when I find myself negotiating with God. I'm prone to wheedle with God, asking questions like: "Do I really *have* to do this? I mean, what's the big deal God? Why does this really matter so much? Why don't I skip this one and I'll make it up with something else."

Or I'll find myself niggling: "Would it really be *sooo* bad if I did that? I won't do that other thing, but it really wouldn't hurt anybody if I went ahead and did this, alright?"

Times like that, when I find myself playing "Let's Make a Deal" with God, as though my eternal destiny was just a big cosmic game show, I have to stop and think, what am I doing? Why am I trying to nickel-and-dime God? It's like I'm trying to drive the hardest bargain with God that I can, attempting to hold back as much of myself as I can. And what I'm trying to hold onto is the thousands, the little human things, when God is offering divine millions—more than I can even imagine. Scripture tells us,

". . . eye has not seen, and ear has not heard . . . what God has prepared for those who love Him . . ." 1 Cor 2, 9.

In *The Weight of Glory* C. S. Lewis wrote:

> Indeed, if we consider the unblushing promises of reward and the staggering nature of the rewards promised in the Gospels, it would seem that Our Lord finds our desires not too strong, but too weak. We are half-hearted creatures, fooling about with drink and sex and ambition when infinite joy is offered us, like an ignorant child who wants to go on making mud pies in a slum because he cannot imagine what is meant by the offer of a holiday at the sea. We are far too easily pleased.

And sometimes the worst thing is that we don't even like the junk we're clinging to so tightly. Sometimes the hardest things to let go are anger, hurt feelings, pride.

Turn it over to God. Giving up our mud-pies, giving up ourselves to let God work in our lives, and accepting what He offers, we can strike the best deal of our lives—because what God wants, what God offers, is *us*: the people we are truly meant to be, in heaven, with Him, in joy so great we can't even imagine it, for eternity. And in the end, that's the only thing that matters.

"A child and a fool imagine 20 shillings and 20 years can never be spent."

Benjamin Franklin in *Poor Richard's Almanac*

19

The Most Important Person

Every child deserves to be the most important person in the world to someone. The ever pithy Lou Holtz, who said of himself: "I'm so old I don't even buy green bananas anymore," once made an observation to the effect of: "80% of people don't care about you one way or the other. 19% of people hope you fail. The other 1% is your family."

I think Holtz got the "indifference to hostility" ratio about right. Most of the world just really doesn't care what happens to you, and it lets you know it. I've heard opining that parents should make sure their kids know they aren't the only pebble on the beach. But spend five minutes on a playground. Of all the items on a parent's agenda, that's one lesson they don't need to worry about. The world teaches kids that lesson all on its own, no input required from parents.

I had our kids out at a park last week and our older daughter, Liz, whose a little over two-and-a-half, went to join two other girls making pies in the sandbox. Liz had a bucket in one hand, a shovel in the other, and a big smile on her face. She was ready for her favorite park activity: playground baking. Her specialty is "seasoning," which involves the careful shaking of specially selected sand over pies as a last, finishing touch.

"Hi," Liz said. "My name's Liz. What are you doing?"

One of the two girls looked up, the other just kept mixing sand.

"Go away," the girl who had looked up said. "You can't play with us."

Then she actually got up and gave Liz the Heisman, standing at the edge of the sandbox with her hand extended in a straight arm to ward Liz off and keep her at bay, lest Liz somehow gain access to their sand-pies.

Liz just stood there, watching the two girls, with her bucket and shovel hanging idly at her sides. No more smile.

"Come on, Honey," I called to her. "Why don't you come here and have a snack with your sister and me."

Liz came over for what solace pretzel rods and apple juice (along with a hug from Dad) can offer. She was alright, though. The chilly breeze blowing from the direction of her potential pre-school playmates didn't phase her much. Those sorts of interactions aren't that unusual on the public park circuit, and, unfortunately, Liz is already used to it. Even before she's three years old.

Early and often the world is sending the message: "*You don't matter.*" "*I don't care.*" "*Don't bother me.*" Indifference shines through most every encounter our little charges have with the big, wide world. They don't need more practice at home in playing second fiddle.

What's needed is for kids to know they really do matter. Someone cares. Someone is glad for their company, is interested to hear what's on their mind, and wants to know how they are. They need to know there is someone who lights up with joy just to see them, and there is someone in the world who, more than anything else, just wants to be with them.

They won't get that from any institutional childcare, formal educational setting, or other pay-for-care arrangement. Their only chance for that kind of experience is from their family.

Modern culture isn't exactly super-inundated with an overabundance of love, growing-up all around us like the verdant green of a rainforest. Borrowing from C. S. Lewis, a parent's task "is not to cut down jungles but to irrigate deserts," so that even traveling through the arid desolation of current civilization, a child will still have the chance to see what love looks like—and learn to nurture it themselves as they grow.

We do that for our kids in a million ways: listening, being open to interruptions, reading to them, foregoing nights out to instead spend time with our little ones, and really being with them—paying attention to them, hearing what they have to say—rather than just inhabiting the same space with them while we check our e-mail and they watch a movie.

In our family, we make it a point to eat meals sitting down at the table together, with no TV, and beginning the meal with a prayer. I was having lunch with the girls the other day (we have a second daughter who's one), and Liz was happily chatting away about what we had been doing that day (we seem to re-cap all of our adventures at every meal), when she looked at me and paused amid the description of the great broom she had found on our walk (Liz loves to find "brooms"—fallen tree branches with lots of leaves still attached—and sweep the sidewalk).

"You like it when I talk?" she asked. "You like listening to me?"

"I love it when you talk, Love," I told her. "I like hearing what you have to say."

It's hard to enumerate all the little moments and all the different ways that every day brings to show love and respect to our little people. But they all begin with the desire and commitment to do so. It reminds me of Jesus' explanation that all of the law and all of the prophets depend on two great commandments: love God with all you have and above all other things, and love your neighbor as yourself. Mt 22, 34-40. If we can keep first things first and stay clear on our principles, we'll be in a better position to work through the rest of the details as they come along.

Still, as Scripture tells us: "God made mankind straight, but men have had recourse to many calculations." Ecc 7, 29.

After Jesus explained the two great commandments, Luke tells us that a man who "wished to justify himself" asked Jesus: "And who is my neighbor?" Lk 10, 29.

Jesus answered the attempt to wriggle around the edges of His words with the parable of The Good Samaritan. A man is robbed and beaten and left for dead on the side of the road. A priest and a Levite both pass him by, continuing on their own way. But a traveling Samaritan stops to help. The Samaritan spends his time and money and gives of his attention and care to tend to the injured man (with no thought of recompense ever mentioned). Then Jesus turns the tables on His finagling inquisitor and asks him: "Which of these three, in your opinion, was neighbor to the robber's victim?" Lk 10, 36. The man knows the answer: The Good Samaritan.

Despite the shifting and beguiling forms that man's calculations can take, truth will out in the crucible of action: pass by the person in need? Or stop to help, despite our own plans and desires and preoccupations?

God has given us all different journeys to make in life, and God places different people in our path for us to care for as we make our way. Starting first, for those of us who are parents, with our children. Our children need us to be their 1%. No one else will, so it's up to us, while there's still time for us to buy green bananas! Besides, sometimes what we take to be detours are the real path, even if we don't realize it at the time.

"There is but one tragedy, not to be a saint."

Leon Bloy, *The Woman Who Was Poor*

Quoted in English (original in French) by Ralph McInerny in *Some Catholic Writers*

20

Virtuous in Evil Times

My grandfather was a hardworking man. Growing up in frontier country out West, he started his career as a carpenter, spent years building barns, then travelled the West as an itinerant farm worker. In World War I he enlisted in the Marines and fought in Europe, including the Battle of Belleau Wood and the Battle of Chateau Thierry. He earned a purple heart and after the war became a gold miner in the Dakotas. When the government shut down the mines, Granddad returned to the carpentry of his youth.

My Dad remembers roofing houses with him. "I never thought about it at the time," Dad said. "But looking back, he was already an old man by then, and there he was humping shingles up and down a ladder all day long, two bundles at a time."

Times were tough, but Granddad was too, and he needed money to feed his wife and kids.

One job he got was on a crew building a new house. When it came time to put on the roof, the wood they were supposed to use was trash. Granddad told his boss. His boss said: "Use it anyway."

Granddad explained that the wood wasn't fit for the job.

"It'll be covered up," his boss said. "No one will know."

Granddad told him he wouldn't do that.

"You'll do what I tell you and use that wood to build the roof," his boss said, "or you're fired."

Granddad gathered his tools and left the job site.

I thought of that when I read in Scripture about Josiah. The Bible tells us: "He turned to God with his whole heart, and, though times were evil, he practiced virtue." Sir 49, 3.

There can be harsh consequences for following the road of virtue in evil times. Real consequences, like a lost job when you need the paycheck. Yet, the consequences of turning aside from the true way . . . well, in *Christ in the City* Father George Rutler related a conversation between Sir Thomas More and his wife, Dame Alice, while More was imprisoned in the Tower of London. Dame Alice pleaded with her husband to just sign the oath demanded by King Henry. As Father Rutler recounted:

> [Thomas More] said "Dame Alice, if I did sign this paper, you say I could enjoy my house and my gardens and my library. How long do you think I could enjoy them?"
> "Oh," she said, "if the Lord is good, mayhaps 20 years."
> "Dame Alice," [More said], "he would be a poor mathematician indeed, who for 20 years, nay 200 years, would risk the loss of all eternity."

In the great and terrible scene of More's trial in *A Man for All Seasons*, More is convicted by the perjury of Sir Richard Rich. After Rich tells the lie which will condemn Thomas More to death, More says: "In good faith, Rich, I am sorrier for your perjury than my peril."

As Rich turns to leave, More says to him: "There is one question I would like to ask the witness. That's a chain of office you're wearing. May I see it?"

Sir Richard shows the chain with its enameled symbol to More, and More says: "The Red Dragon, what's this?"

Sir Thomas Cromwell, the infamous minister of King Henry who was acting as prosecutor against More at the King's behest, and the man who had conspired with Rich to produce the perjured testimony in exchange for Rich's elevation to his new office (an appointment which Cromwell himself made), answers: "Sir Richard is appointed attorney general for Wales."

To which Thomas More replies: "For Wales. Why, Richard, it profits a man nothing to give his soul for the whole world. But for Wales?"

Now multiply the effect; because beyond the salvation of our own souls, there is another dimension to our call to virtue, one of particular concern to those of us with children. In *Prince Caspian*, one of the books in C. S. Lewis's *Chronicles of Narnia*, Lucy is travelling with companions in Narnia when they find their way blocked by a gorge. To one side are steep cliffs, to the other the land slopes downward. Lucy sees Aslan on top of the cliffs, and Aslan wants Lucy to follow him up to the heights. But Lucy's companions don't see Aslan, and ignore her pleas to climb. They choose to follow what seems to them the easier, downward slope; and Lucy goes with them. In the end, what had appeared to be the easier way leads to problems and delay. That evening, Aslan visits Lucy while her companions sleep:

For a time she was so happy that she did not want to speak. But Aslan spoke.

"Lucy," he said, "we must not lie here for long. You have work in hand, and much time has been lost to-day."

"Yes, wasn't it a shame?" said Lucy. "I saw you all right. They wouldn't believe me. They're so –"

From somewhere deep inside Aslan's body there came the faintest suggestion of a growl.

"I'm sorry," said Lucy, who understood some of his moods. "I didn't mean to start slanging the others. But it wasn't my fault anyway, was it?"

The Lion looked straight into her eyes.

"Oh, Aslan," said Lucy. "You don't mean it was? How could I – I couldn't have left the others and come up to you alone, how could I? Don't look at me like that . . . oh well, I suppose I *could*. Yes, and it wouldn't have been alone, I know, not if I was with you. But what would have been the good?"

Aslan said nothing.

"You mean," said Lucy rather faintly, "that it would have turned out all right – somehow? But how? Please, Aslan! Am I not to know?"

"To know what would have happened, child?" said Aslan. "No. Nobody is ever told that."

"Oh dear," said Lucy.

"But anyone can find out what will happen," said Aslan. "If you go back to the others now, and

wake them up; and tell them you have seen me
again; and that you must all get up at once and
follow me – what will happen? There is only one
way of finding out."

The practice of virtue isn't just for our own benefit. It's
also for the benefit of everyone else on the journey with us. On the
radio many years ago a man related a true story about a surprising
encounter he had in a third world country notorious for its rampant
corruption. The man was a frequent business traveler to this
country, and knew how things worked. On one trip he was stopped
by a police officer, as had happened before, and he pulled out some
cash for the standard bribe. But to his shock, the officer refused the
money.

"What?" the man asked in confusion.

"I don't take bribes," the police officer said. "I have
children. I want to leave them a better country."

In his book *Catholicism*, Father Robert Barron noted that
one of the motivations of Peter Maurin in founding the Catholic
Worker movement was "to build a society in which . . . 'it would
be easier for men to be good.'" The decisions we make affect us,
certainly, but they also impact the world around us, changing it for
the better or the worse. Choosing virtue is one way the Lord has
given us to wake our fellow travelers and lead them to follow Jesus
onto the heights. The police officer who refused a bribe awoke a
world-weary businessman. Thomas More's example continues to
arrest the attention of many and lead people toward Christ to this
day, centuries after his rendezvous with an executioner's block.
Every day, in whatever little bit of space and time God has given
us to inhabit, our actions contribute to making the world a place
where it will either be easier or more difficult for our children to
practice virtue.

If we're willing to put our shoulders—small and weak as
they may sometimes seem to us—to the great wheel of our age and
try to nudge it in the direction of virtue, we may be surprised at the
good we can do. In Charles Dickens' novel *A Christmas Carol*,
Jacob Marley said, with wisdom gleaned only from the other side
of the grave, "any Christian spirit working kindly in its little
sphere, whatever it may be, will find its mortal life too short for the

vast means of usefulness." In other words, our problem isn't that there is too little good we can do, but rather that we can do too much, "for this earth must pass into eternity before the good of which it is susceptible is all developed." Our lives aren't long enough to accomplish all the good that can be done from right where we are, right now. We have to seize the opportunities we have now—even (or maybe especially) when they look more like challenges than opportunities. If we don't, then as Aslan said, we'll never know what might have been. And if we do? The answer is waiting for us to find it. We might not learn it here and now, but whether it takes 20 years or 200, eternity will be on our side.

"Never worry about numbers. Help one person at a time, and always start with the person nearest you."

Mother Teresa

21.

Mother's Day

God gives Moms big hearts—because He knows they're going to need them. Especially when the Mom in question happens to live in a family of jokesters.

Take our family, where the Jokester-in-Chief is none other than Dad himself. One time Mom went down to the basement to do a load of laundry and saw a bat clinging to the brick wall. Mom *hates* bats. She ran upstairs, locked the basement door, and waited for Dad to get home from work.

"Oh Honey," Dad said when finally he got home, "don't worry, the bat's probably long gone by now. I'm sure it's fine to go down into the basement."

"Will you go with me?" Mom asked.

"Sure," Dad answered. He got a tennis racket— just in case—then unlocked the basement door and led the way down. Mom followed behind with her basket full of laundry.

Dad reached the bottom first, and when Mom was half-way down the stairs, Dad turned and yelled: "DUCK!"

Mom screamed and threw her hands in the air, sending laundry flying everywhere, and ran back up the stairs.

Needless to say, there was no bat. Just a batty husband laughing so hard he about fell over.

Or the time my brother John was re-wiring an electrical outlet in his room. He was about 17 or 18 at the time, and had already been working construction for several years. Still, Mom was nervous. "Isn't that dangerous?" she asked. "Are you sure you should do it? Maybe it would be better to wait for your father."

"Ah, don't worry," John said. "It'll be fine. The only thing is, if I accidentally touch the positive and negative at the same time, my body could form a circuit and get frozen in the electric current. So if the lights start to flicker, come up and knock me off the outlet to break the circuit."

Mom gulped.

"Don't worry," John said. "What are the chances of that happening?" and he left the room with tools in his hands and an impish grin on his face.

Mom went to the kitchen to make herself a sandwich. While she was busy in the kitchen, John snuck around to the hallway outside the dining room door, and there he silently awaited his opportunity. When Mom finished making her lunch, she brought it, along with her book, to the dining room table to eat, as she usually does. She sat down with her back to the door, and when she got herself settled, opened her book and took a bite of her sandwich, John reached his hand around the doorway to the light switch. He jiggled the light switch up and down, making the lights flicker, and—BAM! Mom shot up like she'd been struck by lightning!

I think it actually scared John a little. None of us knew Mom could move that fast. If John could sneak around inside an Olympic stadium to pull that kind of stunt, Mom would be dripping gold medals by now. As it was, the only thing that saved her from total pulmonary failure was John erupting into uncontrolled gales of laughter. Sorry Mom, but you know it's just our way of showing we love you.

And those were just the jokes. Moms need an aorta of iron even before they get to the hard stuff. Like nights holding a small child burning with fever, or the first day of school. And then there are the problems that can't be solved with a kiss or homemade cookies (though I tell Mom that there really isn't much that can't be cured by her homemade cookies, and I'm always in need of more healing!). As a parent, the hardest things to bear are often those situations in your child's life that are beyond your control. Times when your children suffer disappointments, injustices, and heart breaks. Times when dreams crumble. And times when you watch your children make choices you know they'll come to regret (knowledge we've often gained the hard way ourselves). Times, in short, when a parent prays. We may wish we could do more, but we can't. Besides, in those situations there's nothing more powerful than prayer anyway—and no one prays like a Mom.

I daresay I've done my share to put mileage on Mom's rosary beads over the years. Maybe this year I'll buy her a new

rosary to replace some of the ones she's worn out on my behalf—
though it will probably be more of a gift for me than for Mom,
because I still need those prayers, and I know she's still sending
them my way, every day.

Which is really one of the things about Moms: God gives
Mom's big hearts because Moms need them, but even more,
because He knows that *we* need them. We need all the love and
prayers and sacrifices that flow from the hearts of our mothers.
From the time we're little tots, not allowed to leave the back yard,
to those telephone calls when a Mom can hear the heartache in a
voice all the way across the country. And there's really nothing
we'll ever be able to do repay all the love our Moms have lavished
upon us. All we can do is say, "Thanks, Mom," and let her know
how much we love her—but maybe this year with flowers instead
of practical jokes.

"Don't wish to be anything but what you are – and be that
perfectly!"

St. Francis de Sales

22.

Where there is Life there is Hope

"Success is not final, failure is not fatal: it is the courage to
continue that counts."
Winston Churchill

Winston Churchill purchased that insight with dear
experience. I didn't realize what a rollercoaster of Himalaya-highs
and Death-Valley-lows his life had been until I listened to The
Teaching Company lecture series *Churchill* by J. Rufus Fears.

Turns out that Churchill, the great orator who "marshaled
the English language and sent it into battle" (John F. Kennedy),
spent his childhood with a stutter and speech impediment. Through
hard work he overcame the stutter, but a lingering lisp persisted his
whole life.

And Churchill the great author, who made a fortune from
his many books—and won the Nobel Prize for literature—was a
scholastic flunky. He was dead last in his academic class, which
turned out to be a blessing in disguise since it convinced
Churchill's father (who mercilessly criticized Churchill his whole
life, telling Winston he was a total failure) to accede to Churchill's
desire to join the military, since (as he scornfully declared)
Churchill "wasn't smart enough to be a lawyer" anyway. In his
father's defense, Churchill almost died in 1931 when he was hit by
a car in New York City. Churchill was bedridden for weeks, and he
admitted the accident was entirely his own fault, so maybe
Churchill really wasn't cut out to be a lawyer after all.

But deciding to join the military and being accepted by the
military were two different things. Churchill *failed the entrance
exams* to the Royal Military College at Sandhurst. So he took the
tests again. *And failed a second time*. Not to be deterred, Churchill

went for special tutoring and finally, on his third try, just barely squeaked by.

Then came one of Churchill's highs: at Sandhurst he did well. He graduated and was commissioned a cavalry officer.

Consider that for one moment: cavalry. As in horses. That gives you some inkling of the enormous sweep of changes Churchill witnessed in his life. He began his military career on horseback, and saw World War II ended by the power of the atomic bomb. He lived through the transition from horseback cavalry to men in space. And Churchill took a personal interest in those new-fangled air-machines: he became a pilot himself.

But that was still yet to come. Back in the days of combat from horseback, Churchill saw action from Cuba to Afghanistan to Africa, and distinguished himself for bravery under fire. Once he was in an advance unit on a scouting mission in the mountains of Afghanistan that was ambushed and overrun by a vastly larger enemy force. He barely survived, but managed to rescue wounded comrades, carrying them to safety on his back.

In another engagement, during the Boer War in South Africa, he was on a troop train that was ambushed and derailed. For four hours he worked under enemy fire to get the train back on the tracks, and managed to save many British soldiers. Throughout the whole ordeal, Churchill was so calm under fire that one of the soldiers on the train declared that Churchill was either the bravest man he ever encountered, or the craziest.

But Churchill himself was captured by the Boers and sent to a military prison.

And he escaped.

He didn't know where he was. He didn't speak a word of Dutch. He was alone in Africa. Wanted posters went up showing his face and noting that he could be identified by his speech impediment. But by hook and by crook, through stealth and subterfuge (and a large measure of luck) Churchill made his way across South Africa to British territory and freedom.

The story of his escape was carried in newspapers, and Churchill became a war hero. He capitalized on the fame by running for office. It wasn't his first try at Parliament. He had already run for office once before, in 1899, and *lost*. Churchill the great statesman began his political career with an electoral defeat.

But in 1900, with the fame of his African exploits adding luster to his name, the outcome was different and Churchill won his election. It was another high point. By this time Churchill had published four books, all of which had sold well, he'd been on the lecture circuit, and at 26 years of age he was a self-made millionaire *wunderkind*, and now he was a Member of Parliament.

He began advancing in government and by the time war broke out in 1914 Churchill was First Lord of the Admiralty, a position that put him in the War Cabinet, with heavy responsibility in the war effort. Churchill was aghast at the destructiveness of trench warfare and advanced a plan for a campaign in the Dardanelles, hoping to knock Turkey out of the war and get at Germany through a back-door route that would end the massive bloodletting of the Western Front. But things didn't work out that way. The Dardanelles campaign ended in disaster, with over 40,000 dead and 90,000 wounded.

Churchill's wife said the disaster almost killed Churchill. It certainly killed his political career, or seemed to at the time. He was removed from office and an official investigation was launched against him.

Churchill's response? To go into the trenches himself. Removed from office, Churchill went to fight on the very Western Front which he had tried to render obsolete, and he saw heavy action.

But another turn was on its way. Despite Churchill's political enemies, who must have thought they'd made a final end of him, Britain was at war—and Churchill was needed. Due to bureaucratic ineffectiveness, the British couldn't keep their troops on the front lines supplied with munitions. The Dardanelles investigation had cleared Churchill, and Prime Minister David Lloyd George knew that Churchill was a man who got things done, so in the face of protest Lloyd George brought Churchill back and made him Minister of Munitions. Churchill didn't disappoint. He turned things around at the Ministry and soon armaments were flowing again.

At the end of the Great War, Churchill celebrated victory with his nation, and in the post-war years his responsibilities in the government began growing once more. He became Secretary for War and Minister of Air, and eventually Colonial Secretary.

Then in 1922 another sudden reversal: *Churchill lost his re-election campaign!* And he didn't just lose, he lost huge— coming in *fourth* in the contest for his district's seat in Parliament! It was part of a massive change in voter sympathies that saw Churchill's whole party losing a huge number of seats and beginning to disintegrate. Churchill could forget about high office—he was entirely out of Parliament. And if that weren't bad enough, as an extra kicker he had appendicitis. He quipped later: "Out of government, out of office, I woke to find myself without a seat, without a party, without an appendix."

Churchill didn't wallow in self-pity. Instead, he changed to a new district (in British politics you don't have to be a resident of the district you represent), a new party, and ran again. To no avail. *He lost a second straight election.* So he switched districts yet again, and switched parties yet again—*and lost yet again.* His third straight loss. Still no seat in Parliament, still no appendix. From the 26 year old wunderkind who first entered parliament in 1900, Churchill had become an overweight, 50-year-old, three-time loser.

But Churchill didn't give up. He ran again and on his fourth try he finally won an election. Back in Parliament, he rose again in government, becoming Chancellor of the Exchequer—an important position in British politics that signals a possible future Prime Minister. Only to experience removal from office once again when he was thrown out as Chancellor of the Exchequer five years later, after yet another tectonic electoral shift (but this time Churchill retained his seat in Parliament). After this latest reversal Churchill endured a long period as an outsider. He still had his seat in Parliament, but he was out-of-fashion, out-of-influence, and out-of-favor. These were called his "Wilderness Years." (Fears).

Churchill used the new-found free-time that came with being removed from office to tour America with his son. While aboard a ship crossing the Atlantic, Churchill wrote a letter to his wife reflecting on how wonderful it was to have the financial security that came from their investments in the American stock market. Though Churchill's political career looked to be over, at least with their financial security he'd be able to do the things he'd always wanted without having to worry about money. It was 1929 when Churchill made that Atlantic crossing and wrote that letter. He disembarked in America just in time for the Black Thursday stock-market crash and the onset of the Great Depression—and the end of the very financial security he had just written about to his wife.

It was just par for the course in the strange mix of uncanny timing and odd paradoxes that made-up Churchill's eventful life. Like his unlikely pairing of hobbies: oil painting and brick-laying (among others—he was a man of many interests). Along the way, Churchill had also married, welcomed five children into the world, and suffered the tragedy of one daughter's death from illness at the age of two.

His was a life already well-seasoned in adversity—in guts, grit and glory—by the time the great struggle was thrust upon him when, at the age of 65, he was called upon to lead his nation in World War II.

Those were dark times. Times of despair and defeatism. Times when people were losing hope.

Churchill took over from Neville Chamberlin, the advocate of appeasement who had promised peace by abandoning Austria and Czechoslovakia. Of course, it didn't work out that way. Appeasement didn't halt the Nazi onslaught, and once war was eventually declared, there was a widespread lack of confidence in Chamberlin's ability to prosecute it, and he was forced to step down. In the resulting confusion the names of several possible successors were bruited about.

Lord Halifax was one contender. He was the Foreign Secretary under Chamberlin and another proponent of appeasement. He was also the favorite of the King of England, who, like Halifax himself, believed England could not win a war against Germany and must make terms with Hitler. Their idea was that Britain should let Germany have the European continent uncontested in exchange for Hitler's promise not to interfere with England's overseas Empire. Hitler told Herman Goering: "'England is finished . . . they will make a peace with me.'" (Fears).

But Halifax didn't get the job. Instead Churchill was named Prime Minister. Still, both Neville Chamberlin and Halifax remained in the War Cabinet, and a hard push was made to try to force Churchill to negotiate a truce with Hitler. Denmark had already surrendered, after only a few perfunctory shots. Belgium had already surrendered, trapping British forces at Dunkirk. The French were in the process of surrendering, so quickly and in such large numbers that the Germans couldn't collect all the prisoners.

In the midst of this, Halifax urged Churchill to seek a truce with Hitler. At a meeting of the War Cabinet Halifax let it be known that he, as Foreign Secretary, had already taken the liberty of opening lines of communication through Mussolini so that Britain could negotiate with Hitler. All that Britain had to do was give Mussolini some English naval bases in the Mediterranean, and Mussolini would use his influence with Hitler to help Britain beg for terms. How magnanimous of Mussolini.

But Churchill wasn't buying it. He told Halifax and the rest of the War Cabinet that Britain would fight until "each of us lies choking in his own blood upon the ground." (Patrick J. Garrity, 125th Anniversary of Winston Churchill's Birth, Ashbrook Center).

Then Churchill went out and told the British nation, and the world, in his famous speech: "We shall never surrender."

Churchill said:

> Even though large tracts of Europe and many old
> and famous states have fallen . . . We shall go on to
> the end. We shall fight in France, we shall fight on
> the seas and oceans, we shall fight . . . in the air, we
> shall defend our island whatever the cost may be.
> We shall fight on the beaches, we shall fight on the
> landing grounds, we shall fight in the fields and in
> the streets, we shall fight in the hills; we shall never
> surrender . . .

Churchill gave the British lion its roar back during England's "finest hour"—and it's darkest hour—but his own journey was far from over. After leading Britain to eventual triumph, and shortly after celebrating Victory in Europe Day along with the rest of the British people, *Churchill's party lost an election and he was out of office as Prime Minister*!

Then he was in for ridicule. In 1946 Churchill gave his famous "Iron Curtain" speech, warning of the dangers of Communism and the Communist threat to Eastern Europe. The expert wags of the day considered Churchill's speech laughable. It was ridiculous and farfetched, they said, not to mention alarmist, to suggest that Russia had any interest in subjugating Eastern Europe. Why in the world would the Communists do such a thing?

Churchill also suffered health problems. He had a stroke in 1949. But he kept at it, and six years after losing office he was back as Prime Minister—this time at the age of 76. In 1953 he suffered another stroke and stepped down as Prime Minister, but continued in parliament until 1964. He suffered more financial setbacks and almost had to sell his home, until a group of admirers came together to bail him out. Churchill's death was another of the strange coincidences that marked his life: he died on January 24, 1965 at the age of 90—on the exact same day his father had died 70 years earlier.

This is just a brief thumbnail of the life of a man who said in a 1941 commencement speech: "Never give in. Never give in. Never, never, never, never – in nothing great or small, large or petty – never give in, except to convictions of honor and good sense."

Churchill would understand well the words of Scripture that "for any among the living there is hope . . ." Eccl 9, 4.

Churchill's life shows the power of truth, as opposed to calculation. His example shows that principled determination can achieve a kind of success that unprincipled cleverness never will— even, or perhaps especially, when it looks like the clever path is smooth and easy, and the way of principled determination is rough and full of obstacles. All of the great things Churchill achieved came from principled determination in the face of adversity. Just consider what the world would be like today if Churchill had followed the easy way of surrender that Halifax tried to force him into—a way already made wide and tramped smooth by many others. France and Denmark and Belgium didn't get the peace and security they sought by giving up and giving in. Nor did the appeasers in England, who tried to take what looked like the easy way at the expense of Austria and Czechoslovakia. In the end, taking the hard road of principle produced a victory, preserved a nation, and passed on liberty to their children, despite all the fears and seemingly impossible odds.

Churchill's struggles were written on a grand scale across history, but the same holds true even for those of us whose deeds don't loom large on the stage of world geopolitics. We all face situations everyday where we see what's right, what must be done . . . and we cringe. We can see the blood, sweat, toil and tears that the hard road of principle will require. It will be tough going, and we know it, and sometimes we wonder: is there an escape hatch somewhere?

When it's gut check time, Churchill's example can be a beacon to us, reminding us that the way of principle, hard though it may be, is the only way that leads anywhere we really want to go. And though the odds may be long, where there is life there is hope—and sometimes victory for what is right. So never give in!

"Dear friends, may no adversity paralyze you. Be afraid neither of the world, nor the future, nor of your weakness. The Lord has allowed you to live in this moment of history so that, by your faith, his name will continue to resound throughout the world."

Pope Benedict XVI

23.

Happy Day

A young couple we're friends with received some fancy candles as a wedding present. Imported from Europe, made of real beeswax, aromatic and elegant, the candles are reserved for occasions worthy of their frivolously luxurious grandeur.

This year the husband's birthday fell two days after Easter. Both Easter and the birthday called for the lighting of The Candles.

After two special days warranting candle combustion in near proximity to each other, their son, a few months shy of two years old, got the idea that the lighting of The Candles betokens something special.

After his Dad's birthday, with the house returned to non-ignition normalcy, the son went to the hutch where The Candles are stored and pointed at them.

"Happy Day!" he said, "Happy Day!" and asked his Mom to light them.

European imports or no, who can resist a toddler begging for a Happy Day?

When our friends told us this story, it made me realize how important family traditions are. Just as faith and works go together, so too the outward expressions of our inner life are important, and they are a big part of sharing that life with our families. It's one way we build a common life together as a family. When a day is special—because an event or a person is special, like Easter or a birthday—we show that it matters with those outward manifestations we call traditions. Things like burning a candle, baking a cake, giving presents, hanging decorations, or saying a special prayer.

Every family has its own traditions. Some are daily, like the family Rosary. I know of a family that has dinner together every night and everyone shares one thing from their day that they are thankful for. What a great way to set a positive tone, encourage family members to share with each other, and get some good dinner conversation flowing.

Other traditions are once-a-year events, like the special coffee cake my Mom makes for Christmas every year—and only for Christmas, no matter how much we might inveigle her to duplicate its spectacular culinary wonder on a more regular basis.

Whether nightly or preserved in scarcity, family traditions set a mood. They act as sacramentals of the domestic church, preparing everyone in the family to receive the graces of family love and joy.

Traditions also act as guideposts along the journey of life. Over the years all those little things that make up our family traditions create monuments in memory for our children. Long after our kids have grown and flown, when the days we marked with family traditions roll around on the calendar, the memory of those cupcakes and songs and statues and special prayers that were shared together as a family in celebration of those feasts will surface again in their minds. Our kids will be taken down that memory lane we've all strolled many a time ourselves, a little walk through the past that begins with the thought, "When I was a kid I remember when we used to always . . ." A walk that can lead them to a consideration of the things celebrated themselves. And when they recollect how these things mattered enough to Mom and Dad for them to invest time and effort into doing something special to commemorate them—it may help give them the idea that these things might be deserving of a second look, even if feast days and other elements of the faith may have fallen by the wayside somewhere along our children's journey.

Family traditions make me think of the woman who anointed Christ before His passion. Mk 14, 3-9. She came "with an alabaster jar of perfumed oil, costly genuine spikenard. She broke the alabaster jar and poured it on His head." Mk 14, 3. Some of the disciples were indignant, thinking it an extravagant waste when the perfumed oil could have been sold for 300 days wages and the money distributed to the poor. Jesus disagreed, saying: "Let her alone . . . She has done a good thing for me. The poor you will always have with you, and whenever you wish you can do good to them, but you will not always have me. She has done what she could . . . Amen, I say to you, wherever the gospel is proclaimed to the whole world, what she has done will be told in memory of her." Mk 14, 6-9.

Traditions are the same way. They cost, in terms of money, time, energy, and personal sacrifice. To create and maintain traditions is hard work. Imagination is required to come-up with good traditions. The preparations necessary to make a special day demand foresight and planning. We have to give up other things we would like to do (including sleep) to do all the shopping, baking, wrapping, hiding, decorating, etc., that go into creating a Happy Day. Year after year, the responsibility falls on us parents to keep the special commemorations alive so they can grow into a real tradition, treasured as a family heritage.

Sounds daunting—and it is—but don't worry if you can't do all the things that you'd like for any particular Happy Day—we never can. That's life. There just isn't enough time, energy, money, or opportunity to go around for all the things we wish we could do, to bring to realization all the possibilities we imagine, or to exhaust all the dreams we can dream. (And how boring life would be if ever we did!)

But just because we can't do *everything* doesn't mean we can't do *anything*. Remember what Jesus said of the woman with the alabaster jar: "She has done what she could . . ."

We shouldn't worry about what we can't get done. We just need to do what we can.

Because the traditions are worth the effort. Family traditions are important. Creating a joyful home is important. And that special coffee cake, or that wall hanging Mom embroidered that only comes out once a year for Halloween, they're more than just breakfast or colorful fabric. They are *festivity*. They are the tangible symbols of love and sacrifice—the perfumed oil—that show someone cared enough to make a Happy Day. And that's important, because we have to do more than just love our children, we also have to let our children *know* we love them. Family traditions are part of conveying that message, with deeds as well as words.

Maybe that's why family traditions become, over time, a family heritage—something loved and cherished, and held in our memory the rest of our lives wherever our journey may take us, just like the story of the alabaster jar that is told wherever the gospel is proclaimed throughout the whole world, because they embody the love that is the real treasure of a family.

"The difference between winners and losers is that losers always have an excuse."

Anonymous

24.

Father's Day

What Dad Taught Me

My Dad was cut from the old-school pattern. Growing-up, it seemed his hands were always covered with either sawdust or engine grease. Mom noticed a leak in the ceiling? Dad built scaffolding and re-roofed the house. Chimney needs some work? Dad does masonry. He fixed our cars—and I'm not talking just oil changes and spark-plugs. Maintaining the fleet necessary to keep eight kids on the road required contending with a lot more than that. Think transmissions. Think engine blocks.

One of our cars was an old Dodge Omni. A day finally came when it went kaput, and Dad pronounced its engine unsalvageable. Understand, this was a rare and extreme pronouncement for Dad. Very few things were ever beyond repair in his estimation. Once I called Dad from the side of the road when my truck conked out. He came and fixed it right there on the shoulder of the highway, scavenging pieces from other parts of the truck to repair the engine. He actually took off the tailgate and used the screws that attached it to the truck to secure the alternator back in place. I drove the truck home when he was done. With the tailgate bungeed to the bed.

That's the kind of guy Dad is. So to hear him say that the Omni's engine couldn't be fixed was pretty drastic. Not that the *car* couldn't be fixed, mind you. Just the engine. He went looking for a replacement engine in a junk yard, and ran across a wrecked race car. Dad's a pretty serious fellow, but he does have his whimsical side. He decided to put the race car engine into the Omni.

For days he sweated and muttered to himself under the blazing sun, while a massive chunk of turbo-charged metal dangled at the end of a chain, suspended on an engine hoist, swaying ponderously to and fro. Pry bars were deployed. There was talk of "moving engine mounts" and "expanding the engine compartment." Before it was all over, I think there may have been some good-old-fashioned pounding: pure blunt-force mechanics. I can't be sure—all I know is that in the end, somehow, he got that engine in there.

After that, I always expected to come out one morning and find the Omni titled forward on its front axle, the rear wheels suspended in the air, weighted down by the new engine. And though its center of gravity was definitely shifted forward forever after with that new engine, the car worked—and how.

To get an accurate picture of the resultant creation, keep in mind that an Omni is a compact car—very compact. If you've seen one of those new "Smartcars"—basically a go-cart with a roof—try to imagine it with the motor from a Mac truck. All I can say is: "*Vroom.*" When Dad was done, that thing had giddy-up.

That's how Dad spent his "free-time" (defined as the few hours he could wrest from already sleep-starved nights that weren't used for making money). He had eight kids, after all, and his own business. He married Mom when he was 18 and they started having kids right away. Which meant he started working overtime right away. And as far as I can tell, he hasn't stopped in the 43 years since.

When my sister Agnes turned 21, we all took her out for a drink. Sitting at the bar, I asked Dad: "What did you do on your 21st birthday?"

"I was changing diapers," he said. "We had three kids."

Different people have different reactions to kids. Some re-center their lives around their kids. Others put their kids in orbit around themselves, remaining the center of their own universe, with the kids only satellites circling somewhere out there on the periphery: plan 'em, schedule 'em, just make sure you control their orbit so they don't crash into you and make a crater in your life.

Not Pops. He's taken plenty of knocks in his time, but he lets the heavens keep on smashing into him. He loved running his own business, despite the crazy hours. But the Carter years were tough. Stagflation hit his business like a sledgehammer. Meanwhile, the kids kept growing and college loomed on the horizon. Dad could have kept-on with what he wanted, but instead he packed-up his own dream and went back to work for someone else to earn a steady paycheck for his family. As I've grown older, and had my own experiences with letting dreams go, I've started to get a better idea of what that sacrifice meant. I asked him about it once, and he told me:

"Not many things in life turned out like I planned, but the one non-negotiable for me was always our family, so I guess I got everything I ever really wanted."

After a pause he added, "And somehow I'm lucky enough to know it. In that I'm doubly blessed."

Scripture tells us that God sent some of his mightiest prophets "to turn the hearts of fathers toward children . . ." Lk 1, 17. "To turn back the hearts of fathers toward their sons . . ." Sir 48, 10.

My father taught me that lesson in how he lived every day. Now that I'm a parent, attempting to follow his example in my own life sometimes feels like trying to wedge a race car engine into an old clunker. Dad's heart is big and turbo charged, but my own is a cramped and wheezy little clunker. But Father's Day is a good time to stop and remember. And for all of us kids, it's a time to say thanks. For those of us who are now parents ourselves, memories of our fathers can help renew us as we carry on with the special charge God has blessed us with, and help us to once again turn our hearts toward our families.

"Occupy your minds with good thoughts, or the enemy will find the bad ones. Unoccupied they cannot be."

St. Thomas More

25

The Faith of Our Fathers

Once I was on a plane to Australia. From San Francisco, it's a 14 hour flight. That's a long time to be suspended between the heavens and the deep blue sea. Next to me was a Canadian engineer, on his way to work on helicopters used in Outback mining. About three hours into the flight he pointed out the window.

"Look at the wings!" he said excitedly.

I looked out the window.

"See how they flex!" he said.

To my non-engineering eyes, "flex" seemed to mean a disturbing tendency to whip up and down like an antenna.

"Most people think airplane wings are stationary," he continued. "But on a plane like this they actually have a 24 foot range of motion, 12 feet on either side of the stationary axis."

As I looked, I saw he was right. I wasn't sure where exactly the stationary axis might be, but the wing certainly jerked up and down and twisted in ways I would not have expected.

"You don't know the kind of stresses involved in mechanical flight, especially for these big planes," he said. "It's amazing the wings can withstand it!"

He seemed genuinely enthralled with the engineering feet of modern wing construction. I was less thrilled. It was interesting, I'll admit. I didn't know airplane wings were designed for "flex." We ran into turbulence and I couldn't stop myself from looking out the window. The wings were shimmying and gyrating like a go-go dancer binging on caffeine. Just when I most wanted to believe the little cocoon of my existence was gliding effortlessly above the vast emptiness of the Pacific thousands of feet below, I saw that it was actually dependent on a patchwork of metal sheathing and rivets flapping wildly to stay aloft.

The friendly engineer at my side taught me something new. It just wasn't a lesson I was eager for at that particular juncture. It would be one thing while I was on the ground, contemplating the dynamics of aeronautical engineering in the abstract. But in a plane hit by turbulence above the Pacific with a long way still to go, it was something else. Life seems to work that way, though. It's not a theoretical exercise. It's very concrete, and we have to live it with circumstances that usually aren't as we would choose them.

That has certainly been true of fatherhood for me. When our older daughter was four months old (and before I became a stay-at-home-Dad), I was going to be taking care of her for the day. As we ate breakfast in the morning before my wife left, I started making a plan for the day. My wife watched me scribbling activities on one side of the page with times on the other.

"What are you doing?" she asked.

"Making a schedule for the day," I said.

She laughed.

"What?" I asked.

"Nothing," she said. "You'll see."

See I did. Babies and schedules, I discovered, rarely converge. Our daughter ate when I had nap time scheduled. She napped when we were supposed to be going out for a walk. And big holes were punched all throughout the schedule for the constant, unplanned diaper changes. By the time the day was over, little was left of the schedule but the paper it was written on.

So now I do less scheduling and more going with the flow. There are many circumstances I'd like to re-arrange all the time. Diapers certainly rank high, but even more than that would be sleep. At times the calling to the vocation of fatherhood feels like God's call to Samuel: a voice that woke him in the night. 1 Sm 3, 4. Eight hours of uninterrupted sleep every night would be heavenly. I've forgotten what it feels like to *not* be tired. But instead, the baby wakes up at night, so I do too. I tell myself I'm learning patience. It's a virtue, after all, and I shouldn't complain about the chance to acquire a virtue. Still, if it was up to me, I wouldn't be working on patience at 2 a.m. while trying to sooth a teething baby. Personally, I really think I could make a lot more progress on patience after a good night's sleep, a leisurely breakfast, and a few cups of coffee. But we don't get to choose our circumstances. We just get the call. All that's left up to us is how we respond.

That's where the Bible can help. Scripture is full of people called by God, to all sorts of work, at times when they didn't think their lives were just as they'd like them to be before embarking on a mission from God. People like Jeremiah. When God called Jeremiah, he attempted to demure, saying. "I am too young". Jer 1, 6. Or Zechariah, he thought he was too old. Lk 1, 18, see also Sarah in Gn 18, 13. Or Jonah—he famously didn't want to go to Nineveh. Jon 1, 3. But maybe the most notorious case of arguing with God to avoid the call to mission was that of Moses, who didn't think himself worthy of God's work in Egypt to free the people of Israel. Ex 3, 11. Whatever the reason, none of them thought circumstances were right when God called. But for each of them, God thought differently.

One of the amazing things common to each of these stories is the wonder God works when His people are faithful and carry through with the work He's given them, even if they didn't want to, or think they could, or understand it. And even when they sometimes needed a little prompting or a second chance. God worked through Zechariah for the birth of John the Baptist. Through Jonah for the repentance of Nineveh. And through Moses God worked many miracles and delivered Israel from bondage. Great things happen when God's people are faithful to His call.

It's reassuring. Those of us called to fatherhood have important work to do. When the angel visited Zechariah it was to deliver the message: you will be a father. That's when Zechariah questioned the call he was receiving, saying "I am an old man . . ." Lk 1, 18.

The angel said to Zechariah in reply: "I am Gabriel, who stand before God. I was sent to speak to you and to announce to you this good news." Lk 1, 19.

The power of that statement sends a shiver down my spine: "I am Gabriel, who stand before God." When I first read that, I thought: *Better sit up and pay attention. If Gabriel's got something to say, it's probably worth listening to.* Gabriel was announcing the birth of John the Baptist, about whom Jesus said: "I tell you, among those born of women, no one is greater than John . . ." Lk 7, 28. Gabriel told Zechariah that John "will be great in the sight of the Lord," Lk 1, 15, and went on to enumerate some of the things that would make John so great. One was that John would "turn the hearts of fathers toward children . . ." Lk 1, 17.

Fathers turning their hearts toward their children—it was important enough for Gabriel to care about, important enough for Gabriel to be sent to come and announce, and important enough that it made John *great in the sight of God.* That gives some indication of how much fatherhood matters.

So we fathers have been given a special task, a task that ranks high in the concerns of the likes of Gabriel, John the Baptist, and, as Scripture tells us, the One who sent them both. So we know that fatherhood matters, maybe more than anything else we will ever be given to do in this life.

And we know from living the calling that it's hard work. Sometimes I'm tempted to think that if I could just re-arrange some of the parameters of my life (and of course I only think of the things that are beyond my control), I could do a lot better as a father. Sometimes like Jeremiah I think I'm too young for the task God's called me to and the responsibilities that go with it. But then sometimes I feel like Zechariah and think I'm too old for the demands of keeping pace with high-energy kids. Sometimes I look at another messy diaper and I feel like Jonah: I just don't want to tackle this one. And sometimes I feel like Moses, thinking God could have surely found someone more worthy to nurture the amazing young souls entrusted to my care.

Those are times when it's good to take a step back and listen to Jesus. Fathering can be tough. Worries and frustrations pile up, but Jesus tells us: "Do not be afraid." Lk 12, 7. God loves us, and He's watching over us. "Even the hairs of your head have all been counted," Jesus said, so: "Do not be afraid." Lk 12, 7. As Jesus reminded us, "Can any of you by worrying add a moment to your life-span? If even the smallest things are beyond your control, why are you anxious about the rest?" Lk 12, 26. Rather, Jesus told us "do not worry . . . But seek first the kingdom of God and His righteousness, and all these things [food, clothes, a roof over our heads, and our other material needs] will be given you besides. Do not worry about tomorrow; tomorrow will take care of itself." Mt 6, 33-34. God made us, He put us in this time and this place, and living is now. It was God who called us to our vocation of fatherhood, even with all the obstacles we face, and God will help and sustain us in our work. Amid all the difficulties we face, it's good to remember that it's no accident that we were put here and charged with raising our kids—and that we're not alone in our work.

We also have the example of our fathers in the faith—people like Zechariah and Jonah and Moses—to show us how to be steadfast in our mission. As hard as the road may be at times, each of our fathers in the faith teaches us again and again one of the constant messages of Scripture: we can make this journey if we go with God. Each of the people in Scripture faced their own challenges, just as we face ours. And another thing our fathers in the faith show is that there is a purpose to our trials, even if we can't always see that purpose. Just look at Moses. The obstacles Moses faced weren't ancillary to his mission, they *were* his mission (at least one of his missions). It was through the hardness of Pharaoh's heart, along with all the other difficult and perilous situations Moses faced, that God revealed His nature, His strength, the reality of our absolute reliance on Him, and so many other lessons. And through the witness of how Moses lived and responded to God's call, he passed on the faith and taught countless people about God, down through the generations even to our own age.

Often when we face difficulties, we wonder, "What am I supposed to learn from this?" Well, there can be many things we're supposed to learn, but perhaps sometimes the lessons aren't for us—or at least not for us alone. Maybe sometimes other people are supposed to be learning something from our example in how we respond to those difficulties, like we all learn from Moses. And those other people may just be the ones who watch us most closely, like our kids. It's one of the great opportunities of fatherhood—to bring the faith alive for our kids through how we live day by day. It's a chance to be fathers in the faith ourselves, handing on the treasure of faith to our children, by being fathers of faith.

I've been blessed to know the power of that kind of example in my own life. My parents say the Rosary twice a day, once in the morning before Dad goes to work, and again in the evening before they go to bed. When my parents face tough situations, they reach for the well-worn beads of their Rosaries. Or rather, I should say, they reach for God through prayer. In all the tumult of the economy over the last few years, my Dad was informed his job was being phased out. Facing unemployment, they started a novena. The day the novena was completed Dad got a call and had a new job. Then Mom and Dad started a novena of thanks. I don't know if they learned anything through that whole experience, but I know I did. When a child sees his parents put their trust in God, especially when the chips are down, it makes an impact.

It's a small example, maybe, but life is made of small moments—and faith and character are formed in those little, unheralded moments. Each act of faith is a like a stone dropped in a pool of water, sending out ripples that touch many lives. If we fathers can live with faith, in the moments great and small, we can hope that our acts of faith will send out ripples. The lives that might be touched by those acts of faith include our children. Then we can hope to pass on faith to our kids, that the great things of faith may bless their lives.

"Discipline is remembering what you really want."

Anonymous

26.

Fourth of July

I love the Fourth of July. When we were kids growing up, the Fourth came along every year right in the middle of that blissful, golden time of green leaves, deep shade, and delicious freedom that marked the heart of summer: when we'd been out of school long enough to forget all about it, and the new school year was still so far away it didn't seem real yet. It was the sweet spot, a season of living in the moment, with days of riding bikes and searching for crawdads in the river, reading books of our own choosing on a shady porch (which for me meant lots of *The Great Brain*), backyard wiffle ball every evening after dinner, and catching fireflies at night. And then, just when you thought life couldn't get much better, along came the Fourth of July, with all its wonders of flying flags and flashing fireworks, parades and pyrotechnics.

Anticipation for the Fourth started building early in our family—because our family started building early! We had an annual "Frost Family Fourth of July Race": a pinewood derby type event where us kids built and raced our own vehicles. Originally we started with cars, but as the years went on we branched out to other genres: paddle boats, sail boats, and airplanes.

Dad constructed the racing infrastructure for our family. Years when we were racing cars, he built a big ramp made of plywood, with side bumpers to keep the cars from flying off. It was about 12 feet long, running from the railing of our back porch down to the ground of our dirt basketball court (as Hoosiers—the name by which natives of the great state of Indiana are known—it was required that we have home hoops facilities, so Dad made a backboard that he mounted on the back porch roof, and we had a large dirt court that saw many an epic backyard basketball battle). When we were racing boats for the Fourth, Dad made two long wooden troughs mounted on 2x4 legs. He filled the troughs with water, then, if it was sail boats, we ran alongside the boats and blew air into the sails. If it was paddle boats, we'd just wind up the rubber bands and let 'em rip. And for airplanes, Dad ran two zip-lines from a second floor window down to the garage, so we had about 40 feet of airspace for the planes to duel it out in the skies above our backyard.

Every year the first step in our Fourth of July celebration was a family conference to determine what type of vehicle to build that year. There was generally some vigorous discussion, followed by a family vote to decide the issue. Once the class of racing machine was settled, Dad went to work in the garage cutting a "blank" for each of us: identical blocks of wood roughly hewn to the shape of whatever our vehicles for that year required: hull, fuselage, or chassis. Us kids would then take our stock starter pieces and begin scheming and dreaming, putting pen to paper and pencil to wood as we planned and plotted the transformation of our stock blanks into personalized expressions of high mobility patriotism. For weeks we'd be busy cutting and shaping with rasps and files, coping saws and X-acto knives. Wood putty, the drill press, paint and brushes, graphite and grease, all were deployed in the quest for Frost Family Racing Glory.

Best of all, we got to work in Dad's garage. He kept a box of sawdust under his table saw, to spread on the ground for absorbing oil when he worked on cars, so the garage always smelled of fresh sawn lumber. We would each claim our own little workspace amid Dad's benches and tables, and we'd explore our way through the treasures he had stowed in all the nooks and crannies. There were shelves and shelves of old baby food jars filled with nails and hinges, nuts and bolts, wood beads and pegs and cotter pins. There were drawers full of leather thongs, pots of paint, and odd bits and pieces from various machines Dad had repaired over the years. There were boxes of scrap wood, and the basket of osage orange logs from Grandpa that came from the old homestead in South Dakota and which were special and not to be touched—but we could smell them, and they smelled wonderful! And there were the tools: wrenches, hammers, saws, chisels, sandpaper, drill bits, clamps, and a whole lot more. It was like

Aladdin's cave to us kids, filled to the rafters with wonders waiting to be discovered.

As the Fourth approached, our vehicles began to take shape. It was always interesting to see the myriad and wildly divergent dimensions those identical blocks of wood could assume after being run through the creative gear works of a bunch of little kids. There were really two areas of serious competition: speed and beauty. My brothers Mark, John and Michael were usually the main contenders in the speed category. And I know I've had lots of physics teachers over the years tell me that weight does not matter when it comes to gravity and acceleration: the constant is 9.8 meters per second squared, and the text books all say that a cannon ball and a feather (all things being equal) will fall at the same rate of speed. But in the real world, all things are never equal, and my brothers always managed to wring impressive speeds from their vehicles by aggressive weighting. They would drill holes in their cars and planes and fill them with heavy plugs of metal, and while the real secret could have been in axels and bearings and grease and WD40, rather than the raw pig iron, their metal-muscled bruiser-mobiles always rumbled down the track or zip line with fearsome velocity—not to mention crushing supremacy in the event of collision with other competitors.

When it came to beauty, my sisters usually set the bar. One year Rachel made her block of wood into an open seat roadster, complete with little clothes-pin people with driving goggles and hair made from yarn that she glued into shape so that it appeared to be streaming behind them in the breeze as the roadster rattled along. Another year, when we were making airplanes, my sister Ruth created in miniature the sort of archetypal plane the Wright brothers fabricated at the dawn of aviation: a light frame made from thin strips of wood covered with sheets of cloth stretched over the frame. Working with such slender pieces of wood, I don't know how she did it, but the final creation was really beautiful. Ruth still has it, and it's as impressive today as it was 30 years ago. Actually, most of us still have all our vehicles from those long ago family Fourth of July races, even after all the years and all the moves (and my wife and kids and I have moved five times in the last five years!). Those vehicles were lavished with childhood imagination and ingenuity and steeped in family tradition and the memories of happy summer days. That's the kind of thing you hold on to.

In the midst of all the building frenzy, we'd take breaks for family excursions out into the countryside in search of fireworks and the perfect ear of corn. We'd load into our van and head out onto the county roads, driving down dusty by-ways and beautiful tree lined country lanes that wandered through fields of waving, sweet smelling corn, hunting for farm stands selling the most succulent sweet corn straight from the fields, sold by the farmers themselves under roadside awnings. Dad elevated corn roasting to a high culinary art. Starting with the finest corn the fertile fields of the Midwest were capable of producing, he soaked the corn, still in the husk, in salt water. Then he grilled it over real wood coals, and us kids buttered and salted them ourselves, holding onto the peeled-back husks, until they were dripping golden butter—so good! As for our family ordinance needs, we preferred purchasing our explosives from roving gypsy entrepreneurs operating out of tents pitched alongside the road. Whether we were scouting for produce or pyrotechnics, it was always an adventure full of interesting characters.

Meanwhile, back at the ranch (actually a little house in the city), while us kids worked in closely guarded secrecy to complete our vehicles, Dad was busy putting up the race-course. There would be measurements and sawing, shimmies and much fiddling and jimmying to ensure leveling, pitch and angles were all optimal for racing. And Mom baked, boiled, pealed, marinated and rubbed, turning the kitchen into a hub of savory activity, all to produce our storied Fourth of July feast, which included nothing less than The World's Greatest Barbeque.

I know: them's fightin' words.

Many a questing gourmand has embarked on the Camino de Barbeque, searching for the secret alchemy of barbeque greatness. And many have found their own hard-won secrets to perfect barbequing after years of experimentation, research, trial and error—and tasting! I'm not here to gainsay any of them. I'll only suggest that, much like sanctity, there are many paths to barbeque greatness, and my Mom found one of them—a *really* good one.

I don't know how she did it. I've tried to recreate it, but never succeeded. I only know it required a great deal of advanced preparation. There were chicken legs in ziplock bags full of juices days before the cooking began, and I heard strange talk bruited about of Worcester and vinegar and brown sugar. Maybe the secret lay in cooking with a real wood fire, waiting until there was a great sea of glowing red coals in our stone-lined, dirt fire pit. There could have been some magic in our family's old camping grill, with its generations of built-up backwoods flavors. Whatever it was, the final results were astounding. The chicken meat was tender, falling off the bone, but the skin was crispy, and the barbeque sauce a multi-layered thing of wonder: a blackened outer coating over a thick and gooey inner core. Oh the expensive dinners at fancy restaurants I would gladly trade for one more taste of that backyard wonder!

The preparations continued, gathering momentum as the Fourth approached, reaching a fever pitch in the last few days. Dad would have dozens of ears of corn soaking in big barrels of salt water in the back yard. Cupcakes would pile up as Mom produced her signature Fourth of July treat for the fireworks show: vanilla cupcakes with coconut frosting, toothpick flags, and red, white and blue jelly beans, which we would always consume with copious quantities of ice cream floats made with vanilla ice cream and strawberry pop (continuing the red, white and blue theme). The race track would be going up in the backyard, equipment was being assembled for our various field games, and us kids were putting the final touches on our vehicles.

Then, when the Fourth finally arrived, Dad would be up early to build the massive bonfire required to produce the cooking coals in time for the feast. And all of our vehicles finally made their public debut, as us kids lined them up along the side of the race track, there to be admired by all as we awaited the time of contest.

With our cars on display, it was time for our bicycle parade! Us kids would decorate our bikes with red, white and blue crepe paper, and rubber band playing cards to our bikes to clack in the wheel spokes as we rode, then ride up and down the street, a gaggle of kids resplendent in their patriotic finery (we wore red,

113

white and blue clothes and baseball hats, and had flags pinned to our t-shirts), singing *Yankee Doodle Dandy* as they peddled.

The parade could last a long time, but when we'd finally worn out our clacking cards and our singing voices, we'd assemble in the back yard for the commencement of official festivities. Dad inaugurated our celebration every year with a backyard ceremony. He'd get out his trumpet and start things off with a medley of patriotic favorites blasted in brass (and he could really make that trumpet sing—he used to play trumpet in a rock band). Then he read from *The Declaration of Independence*. It was always moving to hear those words: *"We hold these truths to be self-evident, that all men are created equal, that they are endowed by their Creator with certain unalienable Rights, that among these are Life, Liberty, and the pursuit of Happiness . . ."*

After that, Dad would raise the flag to fly proudly in benediction over our backyard. With Old Glory keeping vigil over our Fourth of July festivities, Dad played *When the Saints Go Marching In* on his trumpet to close our opening ceremony, and then we kids burst into a frenzy of pop-rock throwing excitement: the Fourth was on!

We channeled all that energy into our field games: a hula-hoop contest, sack races, three legged races, balloon toss, egg races (where you carry an egg in a spoon while racing), and an egg toss (and one year my devious mother entered the lists with a secret weapon: a hardboiled egg. She was only discovered when her egg landed—*thud*—in the middle of the open space between the two rows of egg-tossing contestants after an errant toss by her partner, our three year old sister, and the egg cracked—but didn't break! Much laughter ensued.). The balloon toss in particular got to be an event of high drama as we got older. Somewhere over the years, we perfected the art of the moment-shifting scoop catch. And when we did, we ended up launching water balloons into the sky like a *Hail Mary* touchdown pass in the waning seconds of the fourth quarter. Literally, we'd have to move out into the street in front of our house and we'd be hurtling balloons up and down the block, backing up another ten yards after each stratosphere-grazing balloon toss, waiting for that fateful *kersplat!* that would bring the competition to a soggy conclusion.

And so passed a fun day, until, now approaching late afternoon, with spirits already high from all the antics and competitive fervor of the field games, we finally arrived at the main event: the Frost Family Fourth of July Races. Competition progressed in heats, with the top two winners from each race progressing in the "A" bracket, while all others went into a "B" bracket, from which they still had a shot at eventually winning a spot in the final, championship race. Excitement and the decibel level mounted with each round, until it finally hit "ear splitting" as we reached the climax. All the racers from the day lined the track for the final championship race, and when Dad called, "On your mark, get set, GO!!" total pandemonium broke loose. It was 30 seconds of white hot competitive insanity, half a minute of pure thrill, that ended with a new champion for the year.

Then, drained, yet still tingling from the afterglow of it all, and more than a little hoarse, our whole tribe retired to the boards for an outdoor feast spread in a shady glen in our backyard. Every year Dad set up sheets of plywood on wood tresses to make a super long picnic table, with saw-horse benches, on a nice patch of green grass under the maple trees. And there, amid the splendors of nature, we would feast. There were mountains of the incredible barbequed chicken, corn on the cob piled up like firewood laid away for a Klondike winter, buckets of homemade potato salad and coleslaw, baked beans, etc. And while we feasted patriotic music wafted through the open windows from the family record player: *Anchors Away, Into the Wild Blue Yonder, As the Caissons Go Marching Along, The Marine Corps Hymn, This is My Country*, and so on.

As the afternoon grew late, we would disperse to digest and rest-up, and maybe try a few more spins down the racetrack, while Dad prepared the combustibles for the grand finale of the day. As the sun set, we would start loading paper plates with Mom's cupcakes, get our ice cream floats, and assemble on the front porch. When it was finally dark, Dad would begin the fireworks. There would be exploding rockets, whistling wiz-bangers, cascading fountains of light and color, smoke and the smell of gun powder. It was a wondrous sensory overload.

The whole day was really pretty amazing. And now that I'm a parent myself, I can finally begin to appreciate what a gift a day like that is, and how much work and preparation and sacrifice a parent has to put in to give that kind of gift to their kids. Which really, in microcosm, is a paradigm of what the Fourth of July itself commemorates: people willing to toil and sacrifice for another.

The freedom we enjoy as Americans, the freedom that allowed our family to live as it did—including backyard ceremonies, feasts, egg-tosses, and all the rest of it—was a gift given to us by others. Men and woman sacrificed, fought, endured hell, and gave their very lives, in order to bequeath that blessing of liberty to us—and they didn't even know who we were. The patriots who preceded us, who won our freedom and preserved it and passed it on to the generations after themselves, didn't know all the people they were sacrificing themselves for, save that it was for their fellow men. Archbishop Charles J. Chaput, being interviewed on EWTN's *Bookmark*, emphasized that patriotism is "a Christian virtue." Because, he said, "What it really means, patriotism means that we love our neighbors," to such a degree as to "risk your life even for your neighbor." And, Archbishop Chaput said, patriotism is a Christian calling because "that's how God made us, to love one another in that kind of radical way."

I was reading Michael Novak's wonderful book, *On Two Wings*, and was struck with the story Novak related of a forgotten patriot: Joseph Warren. Warren had been a successful and celebrated physician in Boston. He delivered the babies of John and Abigail Adams. When Warren heard that American forces had entrenched themselves on Bunker Hill in the dark of night, he rushed to join them, and he was there fighting alongside his fellow militia men when the Americans broke two assaults from the Redcoats. But as the long and bloody afternoon wore on, the Americans ran out of ammunition. With no more ammunition, the ultimate outcome of the encounter was no longer in question. But a group of patriots remained behind in the entrenchments to face the final British assault, even with no ammunition—to fight bullets with bayonets, in the worst, most brutal sort of hand-to-hand combat—in order to give their compatriots a chance to escape. Warren was among those who stayed behind. He, along with the rest of the men in the trenches, surely knew he was facing death.

And as they awaited the final British attack, Warren addressed his fellow warriors with these words:

> Our country is in danger now, but not to be
> despaired of. On you depend the fortunes of
> America. You are to decide the important questions
> upon which rest the happiness and the liberty of
> millions not yet born. Act worthy of yourselves.

That echo of St. Paul's urging to "live in a manner worthy of the call you have received" is so powerful. Eph 4, 1. The Fourth of July is a day to remember and honor Joseph Warren and the patriots like him who acted worthy of themselves and their calling in their hour of trial, and passed on to us the gift of freedom. We can say a prayer of thanks for them, and pray that they be in Heaven with Jesus, and ask them to help us as we now take up the mantle and shoulder the responsibility of facing the threats to liberty in our own time. Because we, like those that went before us, are also called to the radical Christian love of patriotism. The charge is now laid upon us in this generation, in this time—the happiness and liberty of our own children, and grandchildren, and "millions not yet born," now depends on *us*. Let's look to the example of the patriots who went before us, and ask them to help us to have the strength to act worthy of ourselves, as the sons and daughters of God we are called to be.

"Courage is fear that has said its prayers."

Dorothy Bernard (recounted by Dave Ramsey in his book,
EntreLeadership)

27.

All of God's Works are Good

"The works of God are all of them good . . ." Sir 39, 33. It's true. I've just been surprised at how many were right under my nose that I never noticed, until I started spending time with a toddler.

There's a park overlooking the Mississippi River about a mile from our apartment. Our daughter Liz is 15 months old, and she loves the park, so I take her there two or three times a day. With both the going and coming, I end up walking the same stretch of sidewalk 4 to 6 times a day. With that kind of high frequency traffic over a narrow bit of concrete, I thought I knew our block inside and out. Day after day, several times a day, it's the same buildings, the same lamp posts, the same dip in the sidewalk that turns into a lake every time it rains. But as Scripture tells us, "Beyond these, many things lie hid; only a few of His works have we seen." Sir 43, 34.

When Liz made the developmental leap from stroller travel to bi-pedal locomotion, my landscape began changing. In the days of the stroller, we made pretty good time getting from Point A to Point B. Daddy pushes with a purpose. That's partly because baby's tolerance for riding is limited. She's good for about 15 minutes, maybe 20 with some gusty singing—which is also a great way to perform charity by entertaining random passers-by (although it's probably the passers-by who do the charity— penance even—by letting the singing pass without complaint).

But the determined stroller alacrity is mostly due to 'Type A' personality leanings. Daddy has a strong streak of "stick to the schedule." Each morning starts with a To-Do List, and Daddy likes to see lots of check marks on the list by dinner time.

But the advent of Liz walking signaled the waning days of efficient, linear travel. Why walk in a straight line when there are so many interesting things to see just off to the side of that neat and orderly pavement? There are the "plints" to touch (that's 'plants' for those not schooled in the Language of Liz). Ants to squat down and wriggle our noses at. Birds to chase. Squirrels to call to.

Making my first walk with Liz down our block, with Liz actually walking instead of riding in the stroller, she was off the concrete and into the dirt and grass before I could say "Hey! I just washed those pants!" It was fun to watch her, though, and she even gave me a job: helping her name all the things she saw. Liz would point to something, and I'd name it. Her finger indicated a flower. "Tulip," I'd say, and she'd answer back: "Te-lup," then point to something new. "Pinecone," I'd say. And she'd respond: "Pin-nut." I was like Adam in the Garden of Eden—with an echo (an echo still working on her pronunciation).

And so we continued, pointing and naming. But as Liz made her slow and wending way, veering left and right to explore the wonders of hedge and curb, Daddy started to see visions of a totally check-mark-less day and he could hear the clock tick-tocking in the back of his head as time escaped.

"Come on, Honey," I told her. "We've got to get to the park."

She answered, "Dandie!" and rushed excitedly to a patch of dandelions.

Well, even Daddy knows that you can't leave a patch of dandelions until you've blown all the 'dandie' fluff to the wind.

Tagging along with Liz on her circumlocution of the neighborhood, I ended up discovering things I'd never noticed before, despite all my trips up and down the block. Like an ornamental brick walk, a patch of blue flowers in a grassy sward along the road, and there was even a massive pod of caterpillars all clumped together on the bark of a flowering tree. I'd never seen such a thing.

We never did get to the park. But we had a great walk and a nice long nap afterward. Daddy didn't make the kind of progress through his list that he usually likes, as there hadn't been any time allocated for "Wander aimlessly down the street" in my plan for the day, and our perambulations put us behind schedule. But then I also hadn't set aside time for "Joy and delight, 10 a.m. to 11 a.m." And that's what we ended up with, thanks to a little child's exuberance, a healthy dose of curiosity, and love for the beauty of God's creation.

It made me think of Jesus' words when He said that we must respect our children. Mk 18, 10; Col 3, 21; Eph 6, 4; Mt 7, 12; Mt 22, 39; Gal 5, 14. It can be a temptation for us parents to want to mash and mold our kids into forms we ourselves fashion for them. But they're God's children, made by Him according to His design for His purposes. Ps 139, 13-14; Prv 16, 4; Sir 33, 10-13; Jer 1, 5; Job 31, 15; Ps 119, 73; Is 44, 21 & 24; Is 43, 7; Is 49, 5; Is 45, 11-12; Is 27, 11. The life of a child isn't for a parent to mold, but rather to help unfold.

Part of respecting our children is letting them make their own way, and do what they need to do, without always trying to force them to adhere to our plans, our schedules, and our ideas. All parents know that in time this will mean letting them go. There is a switch waiting for us out there on the horizon, like the switch from the stroller to walking, a time when our children go from clinging to us (and those times can be demanding—remember feeding her before she could feed herself? Or diapers?), to our kids being the ones that *we* cling to. It can be tough for a parent to let kids live their own lives, though we know we have to. That's our job. That's why God put us here: to help them become the people *He* intends them to be.

And to make that happen, long before the kids are ready for us to let them go, we need to let them grow. When they're little, that means letting them be children, giving them the time to be kids—to wander and explore and imagine. It's easier for the parent to have a program and stick to it. But then we lose the moments of serendipity, the discovery of caterpillars and dandies, the moments of grace that God sends us that we could never plan on or own. To our limited adult minds those moments might occasionally feel like wasted time, but it's in those moments that our kids are learning from a Teacher greater than us, developing into the people God made them to be. Just who that person might be is often one of the "many things [that] lie hid," but we can be sure that "[t]he works of God are all of them good," and greater than what we could devise ourselves, if we will let them flourish.

28.

Unexpected Answer

Traveling can introduce you to interesting people. Once I was sitting on an airplane next to a hippie and a Marine. I know, it sounds like a joke, but this is a true story. The hippie was youngish, maybe late 20's or early 30's. The Marine was a grizzled old veteran.

The hippie was traveling between jobs. He was an itinerant worker in the National Park system, putting in 6 months at one park, then moving on to another. Apparently this is a regular way of life for a whole tribe of National Park drifters, traveling around the country from park to park, living in bunk houses. They're limited to 6 months because if they worked longer than that at any one park, they would become classified as "full time employees" and become eligible for benefits. So each park keeps them on for only six months, then they move to a new park for another 6 month stint, rolling along like tumbleweeds from park to park across the nation, nomads working for the park system indefinitely, but never for long in any one place. The hippie talked about the places he'd been, and asked us where we'd traveled.

The Marine answered: "I've been in all 50 states and 119 countries around the globe."

"Whoa, dude," the hippie said. "That's boss, how'd you travel so much?"

"Been a Marine 30 years," he said. "Became an embassy officer. Get stationed all over the world."

"Wow, man," the hippie said. "That's cool. What's your favorite country you've ever been in?"

The Marine looked at him as though it was the craziest question he'd ever heard.

"The United States of America," he answered, in a tone that said *duh*.

The answer to our questions is sometimes an unexpected one, and sometimes right under our nose. The answer to our prayers often works the same way.

I thought about the hippie and the Marine recently when my daughter was clamoring for my attention. I was at the computer, trying to finish something. She kept crawling over to the desk and tugging on my pant leg. When I'd take my eyes from the screen and look down, she'd reach her arms out.

With a sigh, I'd stop what I was doing and pick her up. I'd carry her to the toy basket and try distracting her with a plastic, singing giraffe. As soon as I could get her focused on the giraffe, I'd sneak back to the computer.

A few minutes later I'd feel that little hand tugging my pant leg.

After several iterations of this, I looked down at her and said: "Love, if I could just have ten minutes I could get this done."

She looked up at me.

"Daddy's got important things to do, Little Love."

She reached her arms out to me.

Alright, I thought, *I know when the jig is up.* This time, I turned the computer off. No more trying to placate her with a plastic facsimile of reality. It was time for real attention from a real person.

I picked her up. Her face broke out in a huge smile, she gave a screech and wriggled with excitement.

Then the thought came to me that Daddy did have important things to do, and the unexpected answer was that I was finally doing them.

There's a saying: "What seems urgent is rarely truly important, and what is truly important rarely seems urgent." It's hard to remember sometimes. The urgent things have blaring horns and flashing lights, trying to fool you into thinking they really matter, *and that they must be done right now*. E-mails and invitations and emergencies-de-jour scream out: answer me now! Get on this! Build your schedule around me! They drown out the quieter parts of life, which is the space that the truly important things tend to inhabit.

As fathers we've got to fight the path of least resistance, always tempting us to put-off our kids. Jesus said: "Let the children come to me . . ." Mt 19, 14. And Jesus told us: "See that you do not despise one of these little ones, for I say to you that their angels in heaven always look upon the face of my heavenly Father." Mt 18, 10. Jesus said that whatever we do for one of the least among us, we do for Him. Mt 25, 40-45.

That's the problem kids face: they are the least among us. They're small and weak and inarticulate and defenseless. Sometimes we pick them up and plant them in front of the TV just because we can. With the taller people in our life it isn't so easy, and not just because they weigh more. Because they kick up more ruckus. Squeaky wheels get greased and quiet wheels get rolled.

But we can change that by following Jesus' example and giving our kids time and real attention. When we do, we're not just doing it for our kids. We're doing it for the least among us, and Jesus let us know how important that is—to Him.

"Men go abroad to wonder at the height of mountains, at the huge waves of the sea, at the long courses of the rivers, at the vast compass of the ocean, at the circular motion of the stars, and they pass by themselves without wondering."

St. Augustine

29

Pass the Faith

Those who have encountered the beauty and power of faith want to give that gift to their children. The question is, how?

Well, there's good news, and there's bad news. The good news is that the best way to pass faith on to our children is easy. It doesn't require a Ph.D. in theology or costly catechetical materials. It's as simple as living the faith ourselves, day in and day out. Kids see, they absorb, and through that, they learn.

My brother John is a fireman. He prays the rosary with his family when he's home. But when he's on duty, he has to sleep at the fire station. Our Mom made him a quilt for the fire station that has a rosary pocket—a small pocket tucked in one seam where John can keep his rosary when he's on duty. His kids immediately dubbed it '*The Secret Pocket*,' and they all wanted a Secret-Pocket-Quilt of their own, just like Daddy's. So Grandma fired up the sewing machine and stitched-up quilts for all the grandkids, each one delivered with a rosary 'hidden' in *The Secret Pocket* (and Grandma and Grandpa even made the rosaries—they are a one-couple workshop).

One night when John was gone on duty, his three year old son Adam went to his five year old sister Grace and asked her:

"Gracie, will you say rosary with me?"

"Sure Adam," she replied.

They curled up under their Secret-Pocket-Quilts, got out their rosaries, and Gracie lead Adam through the rosary. Their Mom overheard it all, standing outside the bedroom door listening to little voices say a broken, imperfect—but perfect—rosary, with tears in her eyes.

No lectures required. No DVD's. No bribes. Just an example.

But that's the bad news: passing on the faith is as hard as living the faith ourselves, day in and day out. No formal "lesson" can substitute for the reality kids experience, the truth of what they see in our lives. Everyone with kids knows they come equipped from the factory with a radar for sham. You can't fake it if you want to instill faith in your children. Kids respond to what's real. What we actually live, that's what kids actually learn. As Scripture tells us, faith is a matter of truth:

> "The Lord said . . . this people draws near with
> words only and honors me with their lips alone,
> though their hearts are far from me, and their
> reverence for me has become routine observance of
> the precepts of men . . ." Is 29, 13-14.

That's hard: passing from routine observance, from a faith that's on the lips alone, to actually changing our hearts. But if we want our kids to have the faith, we must live it ourselves. That's the only way it really works. The big things of faith are taught and learned before they can be explained, conveyed before they can be articulated. Things like love. Joy. Hope. Truth. Sacrifice. Trust in God. Children learn these things only by experience, by what they actually encounter in their parents and homes and lives. The explanations are for later. Explanations are the sculptor's chisel, chipping and refining to bring forth form and definition, but which first requires the stone to already exist. Experience is the stone.

So our task is as easy as living the faith ourselves—and as hard as living the faith ourselves. Day by day, in moments large and small, when no one is looking. What we have tucked in 'The Secret Pocket' of our heart permeates our life, is absorbed by our kids, and becomes part of their life. For our kids to have the power and beauty of faith in their lives, we need to make the power and beauty of faith a part of our lives.

"Why fit in when you were born to stand out?"

Dr. Suess

30.

Planting Seeds

Growing up, we were eight kids, a Mom and a Dad, and the occasional stray cat, in a tiny 3 bedroom house. With one bathroom. And no shower. There was Mom and Dad's room, the boys' room, the girls' room, and a long line for the bathroom. Quarters were tight, but fun was plentiful.

Still, Mom and Dad thought their kids should have some kind of personal space. So Dad made each of us a "Treasure Chest": a wooden box made like a miniature pirate's treasure chest, the kind you see in movies buried on desert islands where "X" marks the spot. They weren't big, maybe twice the size of a shoe box, but they were nice and we each had our very own. No one was allowed to open someone else's Treasure Chest, and each of us even got a lock to secure our Treasure Chest. The locks were only little tin trinkets from the dime store, each with a tiny, wafer-thin key. Nothing that would hold-up against a pen-knife and 30 seconds of prying, but it was the principle that counted. Within the Treasure Chest was our inviolable domain, where we could store our most cherished possessions. Like my souvenir pennies stamped "Pocono Mountains" by a penny-press at a family reunion, and the polished rocks from South Dakota that were my Dad's when he was a kid.

Well, it was 30 years ago (or more) that Dad made the Treasure Chests, but just recently one came to light. Mom was cleaning-out an old closet and found one. It was locked. Talking to my sister Ruthie on the phone she mentioned the Treasure Chest.

"In the closet in the back room upstairs?" Ruthie asked.

"Yeah," Mom said.

"It's mine," Ruthie said.

"Are you sure?" Mom asked. "I was going to open it to find out whose it was, but it's locked."

126

"I'm sure," Ruthie said. "I've got the key, so don't break the lock."

"You've got the key?" Mom asked in amazement.

"Yeah, it's right here on my key ring."

Only Ruthie. Understand, Ruthie moved out of my parents' house decades ago. She's now a mother herself, and a scientist with a Ph.D. in some branch of physics which she's explained to me dozens of times, but that I still don't understand. She works in a fancy lab with ID badges and security codes, making some kind of space-age materials the name of which she's also told me dozens of times, but that I still can't pronounce, and whose uses have also been explained to me on innumerable occasions, but which I still don't understand. After all these years, Ruthie is still carrying the little tin key to her Treasure Chest amid a jumble of industrial grade lab keys and secure-entry swipe fobs.

When Ruthie went home, she produced the little tin key and opened the Treasure Chest. Within were her childhood treasures, including a "My First Science Kit" that had been well used and carefully stowed and was still well preserved.

It reminded me of Jesus' description of the Kingdom of Heaven: it's like a mustard seed. It's the smallest of seeds, but, Jesus said, "once it is sown, it springs up and becomes the largest of plants and puts forth large branches, so that the birds of the sky can dwell in its shade." Mk, 4, 32.

As fathers, one of our tasks is to plant seeds for our children. Seeds of imagination and possibility that can take root and, with love and encouragement, flourish. Small beginnings, like a "My First Science Kit," in time can grow into something we can't imagine now. Most of us won't get the chance to see into our kids' childhood Treasure Chest years later and learn what those seeds of possibility meant to them. But those seeds are the real treasures of childhood. They are the memories our kids carry with them, like little tin keys, into adulthood. They are the beginnings of their future. And there's one seed that's more important than any other: "the words of eternal life," which Jesus alone has. Jn 6, 68. If we can help that seed take root, if we can nourish and cultivate it, then when our kids leave home hopefully they'll have the Keys of the Kingdom to take with them.

31.

The Fuller Brush Man

I admit there were times growing up when us kids rolled our eyes at the strange ways of Mom and Dad. The Old Coots (as they are sometimes known) could just be *so* . . . out-of-step with the times.

Granted, this was partly due to circumstances. My folks raised eight kids in the seventies, which were decidedly difficult economic times. On top of that, Dad was self-employed, which presented extra financial challenges. They couldn't count on a paycheck every Friday. As the saying goes, Dad had to kill what he (and we) ate.

But Mom and Dad were pretty hardy folks. I never knew them to blink when staring uncertainty in the eye. Reach for their Rosary beads, yes. Fear, no. Such is the power of faith.

Through it all the Old Coots learned to stretch a dollar like an accordion at a polka festival. DIY was their credo—from Mom making clothes to Dad turning out furniture in the garage. Cars to composting, Mom and Dad had every facet of the domestic economy covered with the efforts of their own capable and calloused hands. They belonged on a Conestoga wagon opening up new territory, not the shag carpet world of 1970's American suburbia.

Then, just when you thought you knew what made them tick and had every idiosyncrasy of the Old Coots figured out, they would go and throw a curve-ball at you. A case in point was their dogged devotion to the Fuller Brush man. When the Fuller Brush man came knocking at the door, all of Mom and Dad's thrifty pioneer ways went out the window.

For those who don't remember, or are too young to have experienced it (I hate dating myself like this), the Fuller Brush man was an exemplar of that by-gone institution of Americana: the traveling salesman.

The Fuller Brush Company manufactured, as the name suggests, various types of brushes used for household cleaning and personal beautification. They sold their wares through the auspices of the door-to-door salesman. The Fuller Brush man would knock on your door carrying a suitcase full of samples from which he would extract various bristled products, extolling the myriad virtues inherent in the unique curvature and prickly rotundity of each, while giving you a chance to handle these marvels of modern engineering which, thanks to the Fuller Brush man, were available for you to own and use in your very own home. He'd take your order, then return a few weeks later to deliver the goods right to your door. And of course, while he was there, could he show you a few new items that might interest you? All of your brush needs, from buffing the bowl of your toilet to curling the coif of your hair, could be supplied from the same handy itinerant dry-goods retailer right in the comfort of your own living room. It was kind of like today's on-line, internet shopping, only with a handshake and a check instead of the click of a mouse and a Mastercard.

Which was all well and fine, but what puzzled us kids was why Mom and Dad went for it with such capacious profundity. They bought mountains of combs, bristling boxes of brushes, and cleaning implements whose uses I never fully understood.

Don't get me wrong. The Fuller Brush man always seemed like a nice guy. He had a huge smile, he'd chat and joke and laugh with us kids and fill the whole house with the smell of his aftershave. But nice or no, here Mom was knitting hats for the winter and Dad tearing out walls to get at the pipes so he could fix our plumbing himself, and then they'd buy Fuller Brush merchandise like they were survivalists with a serious streak of neat-freak, stockpiling against the threat of a brush-production catastrophe striking the Free World. To this day our family is still drawing down the surplus of Fuller Brush paraphernalia built-up in those years.

Well, whatever it was that made Fuller Brush products so irresistible to Mom and Dad remained an enigma to us, their progeny. It was only when Dad ended-up taking a job in a distant city and our family moved that the Fuller-influx stopped and the Fuller Brush man passed from being a regular household visitor to a memory of childhood days-gone-by.

Until, many years later, after college and law school, I took a job that brought me back to our old hometown. One day I was sitting on a bench in a park where I used to play as a kid, when who should pedal past me on a bike? He was older, a little more bent, with a lot more gray in his hair, but the smile was the same—and there was no mistaking the aftershave. It was the Fuller Brush man.

I couldn't believe it. A forgotten piece of the past brought back to life on an aged and rusty easy-rider, old-folks bicycle. And then, just like that, in the moment of recognition he was already past and gone again in a flash of whirling spokes with only a trailing wisp of aftershave to prove that he'd really been there.

I called Mom that night and told her of my encounter with a childhood icon from yesteryear.

"He was always such a nice man," Mom said. "It's just too bad what happened."

"What do you mean?" I asked.

"About his wife," Mom said.

"What about his wife?" I asked. "I never heard anything about the Fuller Brush man's wife."

"He wasn't always a Fuller Brush man," Mom said. "He had five small children when his wife died. He quit his regular job and became a Fuller Brush salesman so he could have a flexible schedule to take care of his kids, to be home with them in the mornings and after school. It was hard, but he's a good man."

I never knew.

All those years, I'd put down Mom and Dad's Fuller Brush frenzy to a loose cog in the Old Coot wheel-works. But no, as with everything else, they had their reasons.

I was reminded of Scripture: "The intention in the human heart is like water far below the surface . . ." Prv 20, 5.

Parents especially, I've learned, are driven by intentions that can seem inscrutable. Particularly from the view of today's prevailing culture, with its strong emphasis on "me." Whether it's a Dad who trades in a more lucrative 9-to-5 job for something flexible to allow time with his kids—or two Old Coots constantly fiddling with and patching a clunky washing machine dating from the dawn of the Industrial Revolution so they could save some money which they would then turn around and spend on untold dozens of cleaning brushes—those entrusted with the care of God's children (and their allies) have their own reasons for the things they do. If those reasons seem out-of-step with the modern zeitgeist and its "ethic-of-I," it's no failing on the part of the Old Coots or the Fuller Brush men. The prevailing culture is what needs changing. Even the decision to have kids now seems baffling to many. But if our society can be brought back to a respect for life, to again value and honor every human person as intentionally created by God and stamped in His own image and likeness, it will be from the unrecognized and unheralded spiritual pioneers quietly blazing their own counter-cultural trail through the wilderness of modern times, knitting their own hats and fixing their own cars and buying scrub brushes as they lead the way.

"I'm not afraid to fail . . . I'm scared to death of dying and having the Lord say to me, 'Angelica, *this* is what you might have done had you trusted me more.'"

Mother Angelica

32

Now is the Time

My brother John has a great photo from the birth of his first child. It's a picture of his daughter's unbelievably tiny baby-hand gripping his finger. His daughter's whole hand, so perfectly formed and so amazingly small, can only just wrap around John's bony knuckle. You just can't conceive how they can be that little.

John has the same photo for babies 3 and 4, but not for number 2. I told him how much I loved that picture, and how I wanted a photo like with our first baby, who we were then expecting.

"Take it right away," John warned me. "They grow so fast, you won't have long. We waited with Pete and missed our chance."

Well, when Liz was born we didn't take the photo right away. We were tired. It was busy in the hospital. There were phone calls to make (and I've got 7 siblings). We figured we'd take the photo later.

It turned out John was right. By the time we finally got around to attempting the photo, the moment was gone. She'd already outgrown that stunning new-baby tininess.

I was reminded of Jesus' words when He said: "The light will be among you only a little while. Walk while you have the light . . ." Jn 12, 35.

It has already surprised my wife and I how, in just 10 months, we've seen so many stages come and go. There was the immobility stage, when you could count on finding Liz where you left her. That was nice. There was the sleeping phase, when she slept 20 hours out of every 24. That was nice, too. She used to curl up like a little peanut on my chest and sleep while I rocked in the easy chair. My wife and I are always trading memories like that, saying, "Do you remember when Liz used to . . ." It seems every stage has already passed by the time we realize it was a stage. So many memories packed into 10 months, it feels like it's been a lifetime.

I guess for Liz it has been. It's just going so fast. The missed photo made us realize that. There is an old saying coined by Hodding Carter: "There are only two lasting bequests we can hope to give our children. One of these is roots; the other, wings." I don't want to miss anymore photos, but even more than that, I don't want to miss the chance to help Liz form strong, healthy roots. The photos are great, but as a father, the important work isn't digitally documenting her different stages. The important work is nourishing that tender soul as she grows through these stages. And now is the time to do it. She's growing right now. We can't put it off, or, just like the picture, the moment will be lost.

When she's older it will be time to work on the wings. But the roots come first. And she's watching, listening, absorbing, all the time. Now is the time to teach some of the most important lessons. Right now she can feel love. Peace. Joy. All the things we most want for our kids can be learned right now, if we show them. She learns patience when we take the time to feed her, one little spoonful at a time (usually with about a 2/3 delivery success rate). She learns caring when she tugs on our pant leg and we stop what we're doing to pick her up. She learns joy when we play with her. She learns peace when we do all these things with good cheer, not as a chore or a bother, but with a spirit of love.

The sun is shining, so we have to get on with our work while we can. It's for our own good to teach her now anyway. If we wait until it's time for her to get her driver's license, we'll *all* regret it. Those days will have challenges enough of their own, even if she gets strong roots now. The wings are always hard, but good roots can make that stage easier when its time comes.

"No talent can survive the blight of neglect."

Anonymous

133

33.

No Power Hour

My wife noticed that our family suffered from "Computer Creep." Those few hours after work, when we try to squeeze in dinner and time with our daughter before she goes to bed, were being encroached upon by computers. It starts with checking e-mail, then you just need to respond to that one e-mail real quick, then . . . well, if I could just finish up this one thing . . . Next thing you know your wife is interrupting you so you can kiss the baby goodnight before she's tucked in.

My wife decided to institute a new family policy: the No Power Hour. Between 5 p.m. and 7 p.m. (I know, this is actually two hours, but 'No Power for Two Hours' just doesn't have the same ring), no one is allowed to use any device requiring a non-human source of power. Bikes, ok. Computers, *verboten*. Books, ok. TV, *auswerfen*. *Scrabble*, ok. Blackberries, *'raus*. (My wife also speaks German, hence her bi-lingual policy pronouncements.)

The No Power Hour has been a good tool. It's not really computers or TV's that are the problem. Priorities are the problem. But the No Power Hour is a quick reference to remind us of proper priority ordering. Which means family first.

And not just in word, but in deed. When we're tempted to check that e-mail once more, or flip through the channels to catch a score, the admonition of the "No Power Hour" looms before us. Scores have to wait until after Liz goes to bed.

Straightening out priorities and unplugging for a few hours has yielded rewards. The other night, instead of sitting at the computer, I was sitting on the floor reading a book to our daughter. She's only ten months old, so she doesn't really get it yet, but she likes the pictures. As we turned the pages, she gave me a hug. She wrapped her little arms around me, put her head against my chest, and said "Dada."

Wow. No e-mail that can compare with that.

I was reminded of what Jesus told Mary and Martha. Jesus came to visit, and Mary sat at His feet listening to Him speak. But Martha was too busy with chores. Jesus told her: "Martha, Martha, you are anxious and worried about many things. There is need of only one thing. Mary has chosen the better part . . ." Lk 10, 41-42.

Whenever I hear that Bible passage, I always wonder, *What was Martha thinking!?!* You have *Jesus* in your house, the chance to hear the words of Eternal Life spoken directly by Jesus—God Himself!—and you pass on that *for chores*!?! But then when I look at the choices I make, I can understand Martha. She probably just wasn't thinking about it. Just like we don't really think much about how we spend our time. No one consciously decides "I'll watch TV rather than spend time with the kids." We just turn on the TV, and unconsciously fall into a choice. Plus, Martha probably never considered how her time with Jesus was finite. She may not have had the realization that a day would come when Jesus wouldn't be around to stop in for a visit.

The same is true for us fathers. The time our kids are home with us is finite. Their time as children is finite. They are growing-up right now. There will be school, sports teams, friends, then a driver's license, then they're gone.

Not that that's a bad thing. After all, we want our kids to spread their wings, live their own life, and go out into the world to do what God made them to do. Those are all good things—that's the goal. We just need to be aware that the time we have with them as kids is limited, and appreciate it while it's here.

I wonder about Mary and Martha in the years after Jesus' crucifixion. Mary had the memories of her time with Jesus, sitting at His feet, listening to His words. Could Martha remember what had seemed so pressing that day when she just couldn't stop to listen to Jesus? Did she regret what could have been? I know I won't remember what was on TV when Liz was a baby, or the supposedly urgent e-mails. But I will always remember those little arms hugging me, her head against my chest, and the love and joy expressed in a child's voice as she said "Dada." The better part is there for us to take, if we will. The choice is ours.

34.

Rocky Mountain High

Did you ever find yourself in one of those situations where you stopped and thought, *how did I get here?* Once, it was 3 a.m. and I was in the passenger seat of a car on a nameless stretch of road somewhere in the mountains of Colorado, in the middle of a torrential rain storm. This was back in my single days, when I could have slept if I'd wanted to, but for some inexplicable reason I never did. Opportunities lost!

My friend Tom drove while I looked out the window into utter blackness. Two feet from the side of the road was the sharp edge of a 4,000 cliff. Flashes of lightning illuminated the chasm of abyss gaping wide just on the other side of the guard rail. Booming thunder made the whole car shake, and the road wound in precipitous curves as it cut back and forth across the mountain.

Times like these I start asking myself questions. Like, why didn't we check the weather before we started driving? Why didn't we stop at a hotel? How's my life insurance?

As I "pondered weak and weary," over many a mistake I'd made before, suddenly there came the thought—oh no, here's one more! (*The Raven*, Edgar Allen Poe.)

"Hey man," Tom said, "do you ever try to guess which way the road'll turn?"

"What?" I asked.

"I can't see anything at night," Tom explained. "I really need glasses. Usually I can only drive at night by the reflections off the lines on the side of the road. Too bad there are none here."

I looked. Indeed, there was only darkness at the side of the road: no lines painted to help you see where the road ended.

"I try to guess which way the road'll curve," Tom continued. "You ever do that?"

I swallowed hard, my knuckles white as I gripped the door handle.

"No," I croaked weakly.

"Anyway," Tom said, "you better get some sleep. It'll be your turn to drive in a few hours."

Somehow sleep eluded me after that.

Instead of blissful rest, I found myself whiling away the hours playing Tom's game: trying to guess which way the road would curve. Or rather, which way Tom might guess the road would curve.

Since embarking on the adventure of fatherhood, I've had occasion to remember that night. Fathers spend a lot of time trying to figure out what's around the next bend. Sometimes I actually think I've got things figured out, usually just before everything goes cattywampus. I thought I cracked the code for getting Liz back to sleep when she woke at night: feed her the bottle. It was like clockwork. She cries, you get her, change her diaper, and get a bottle in her mouth as fast as you can. Sleep was sure to follow moments later. It was great—until the advent of teething. Then all bets were off. Just when I was sure the road would zig, it went and zagged on me.

I remember my brother John talking about one of his surprises after his first child was born. He works construction, and he told me about driving home one day with his arm hanging out his truck window. Another car went by a little too close for comfort.

"Suddenly," John said, "I yanked my arm in. I thought, I've got to be careful. I need this thing. What if I get hurt and can't work?"

Worrying is an occupational hazard for fathers—over matters small and large. There's the new-found awareness of cups too close to the edge of the table, and breakable objects placed on end-tables or shelves or anything else within two feet of the floor, where little hands can reach. Then there are the imponderables, like what's going on with the economy? Where are those adjustable mortgage rates headed? How much longer will our cars last? As Francis Bacon said: "He that hath wife and children hath given hostages to fortune . . ."

But when concerns about money and mortgages and mileage start piling up, Jesus tells us: "Do not worry . . ." Mt 6, 25-34.

When it comes to food and clothes and material things, Jesus said: "Your heavenly Father knows that you need them all. But seek first the kingdom of God and his righteousness, and all these things will be given to you besides. Do not worry about tomorrow; tomorrow will take care of itself." Mt 6, 25-34. Jesus said: "Look at the birds in the sky; they do not sow or reap, they gather nothing into barns, yet your heavenly Father feeds them. Are not you more important than they?" Mt 6, 25-34. Jesus told us God knows and loves us: "Even all the hairs of your head are counted. So do not be afraid . . ." Mt 10, 29-31.

It's a tremendous assurance.

It's also a tremendous challenge.

We've got to redirect our energies. It's another surprise, another zag in the road, one that runs counter to the worldly messages bombarding us. Jesus said: ". . . seek first the kingdom of God . . ." Instead of getting wrapped around the axle about money, we should devote attention to whether we're doing God's will. Next time we find ourselves laying awake fretting over bills, we ought to stop and force ourselves to take stock of our souls. When was the last time we made an examination of conscience? Rather than tracking the Dow Jones Index, how are we doing on the honesty index? Have we been kind, generous, patient, courageous? Do we bear witness as we should? Are we the example our kids need? Are we helping our wife get to heaven? God loves us and is watching out for us, so let's relax the white-knuckled grip on the journey of life and invest some care into something more important than bank balances: seeking the Kingdom of God.

"Someday is made of a thousand tiny nows."

Leigh Sandley

138

35

Back to School with Saint Joseph of Cupertino

It's back to school time, and for me that means one thing: Saint Joseph of Cupertino. Not a name you usually hear when it comes to books and saints. There aren't many schools named after Saint Joseph of Cupertino. But that's only because it's the people who *give* the tests that name the schools. If the *test-takers* were in charge, Cupertino Academies would be everywhere. He's the patron saint of those taking tests, even though—or perhaps particularly because—he wasn't much of a scholar himself.

Most of Saint Joseph's academic experience was in the school of hard knocks. As the saying goes, he wasn't "the sharpest tool in the shed." A phrase particularly apt for Saint Joseph, since he was born in a shed and lived (for a time) in an animal barn. Poor and hungry as a child, he was sickly and awkward. His school record was dismal, and he lacked any compensating gifts to off-set his academic shortcomings. He wasn't funny or athletic, attractive or affable. Just nervous and prone to staring off into space. After leaving school, he was apprenticed to a shoe-maker, but couldn't learn a trade either. And his peculiar habit of abstraction continued. At odd moments he would simply stop whatever he was doing and stare into space, transfixed by something only he could see, deaf and dumb to the rest of the world. Not a good habit if you're trying to get ahead in the hustle-bustle world of commerce.

He also tried numerous times to join a religious order. Saint Joseph felt called to consecrated life, but with his ignorance, slow wits, and lack of any discernable talents, no order would take him. Until a community of Franciscans near the Italian town of Cupertino finally had pity on him. They wouldn't let him become a friar, but he could sleep on a plank in the barn if he would tend the animals. Joseph accepted, and he was happy. In fact, he was so full of joy, so humble, and so eager for any task the Franciscans set him to, no matter how onerous or disagreeable it might seem to others, that the friars began to see piety where before they had seen only pity. They asked Joseph to become a Franciscan friar and priest.

It was Joseph's dream, and he did his best. But no matter how the Franciscans tried to teach him, and no matter how Joseph tried to learn, he just couldn't get anything into his head. Except for one thing. Joseph had an uncanny and deep insight into just a particular few of Jesus' words recorded in the Gospel: "Blessed are they who are poor in spirit . . ." When it came to that one Beatitude, Joseph spoke with power. Otherwise . . . well, there didn't seem any way Joseph could possibly pass the oral examination by the Bishop that was necessary for ordination. But there was also no avoiding it. He must be tested to continue on the road to ordination, so ill-prepared as he was, the Franciscans sent Joseph to the Bishop for testing, sending him with their prayers—and their breath held.

When Joseph appeared for his test, he stood before the Bishop, waiting. The Bishop opened his Bible at random, and let his finger fall on whatever lines chance (or the Holy Spirit) might dictate. The Bishop looked at the line where his finger landed, then said to Joseph:

"Tell me about 'Blessed are they who are poor in Spirit.'"

Joseph began, and continued until the Bishop finally held up his hand to stop him. No further examination was necessary. Given the depth of Joseph's spiritual insight on this great Beatitude, it was obvious to the Bishop that Joseph was well qualified for Holy Orders.

Against all odds, Joseph had passed the test!

It wasn't quite the end of the road for him, some twists and turns still awaited Joseph, but he was ultimately ordained. And he proved a remarkable priest. A great confessor, he was gifted by God to know the thoughts and hearts of others. He might not be good with books, but he could read souls. And kids love St. Joseph because he could fly and talk to animals.

But perhaps most amazing of all was that strange habit of abstraction. It turns out that St. Joseph had a special grace of being able to see the hand of God at work in the world, sustaining creation moment to moment. It was the beauty and awe of God's involvement in the tiny details of daily life that would overcome St. Joseph, filling him so completely that he was lost to all else.

Today he's the patron saint of test-takers. I love him all the more for his lack of brilliance. Don't get me wrong, I love St. Thomas Aquinas (my wife and I met on his feast day) and all the other Holy Scholars. I marvel at them. But part of why I love Saint Joseph is that he wasn't one to marvel at, at least not for academic prowess. I can relate to that. Even we, the less than brilliant, have tests we need to pass.

When we do, St. Joseph of Cupertino is a go-to saint. In those pressure packed moments, when time is short and stakes are high, St. Joseph is a great intercessor to seek God's assistance. And then after the storm has passed, Saint Joseph is a great saint to remind us that God is still at work in our lives in the small moments, in all the everyday, ordinary-yet-extraordinary things of the world He created.

"Dear God, be good to me,
The sea is so wide and my boat is so small."

Prayer of the Breton Fishermen

36

Well Met

Have you ever wondered how many people you'll meet in your lifetime? I was on a road trip with my wife and kids last week and we stopped at *The Worlds' Loneliest McDonald's*. I've also been to what local urban legend reputes to be *The World's Busiest McDonalds*. It stands all alone amid the never ending traffic of the Chicago Skyway—six lanes that carry nearly 20 million cars a year, hundreds of feet in the air above Calumet Harbor on the shores of Lake Michigan—with no other restaurants on the Skyway. Fast food restaurants "fish from the stream," so the saying goes, as opposed to being "destination dining," and I guess with a lot of fish in the stream you catch a lot of customers.

Well, *The World's Loneliest McDonald's* is the polar opposite of its bustling Skyway brother. It also stands all alone, but not on a fast flowing river of concrete. Instead it's perched in solitary bliss on an island of grass carved out of a vast ocean of corn somewhere in the Midwest. I'm not sure exactly where, since I was using the GPS on a long-haul drive across country. Ever since I got comfortable with the GPS I've stopped looking at maps. I know, it's not a good thing and I'm not proud of it, but it's true. In the old days I'd study out my routes, keep track of mile markers, note exits, and generally stay abreast of where I was in my journey. Not anymore. Now I just get in the car, enter the destination, and let the GPS do the rest. It gives me turn-by-turn instructions and a running calculation of our ETA. It's pretty amazing, but the down side is that anymore I only have a hazy idea of where I am at any given moment, or where I've been.

But wherever it was, we were chugging along a deserted highway in the middle of nowhere when we saw the improbable sight of Golden Arches rising above waving fields of corn. Just at that moment the kids were cranky and nature was urgently calling all of us, so our diminutive band of road weary wayfarers was filled with joy at the beckoning neon promise of clean bathrooms, a chance to stretch our legs, and a tasty repast seasoned with secret sauce.

Forget the Skyway's six lanes of zooming interstate congestion, this little outpost of the globalized economy was tenuously tethered to the highway by a humble access road bereft of even so much as a stop light. I've never experienced such a quiet and bucolic setting for a fast food restaurant. We were hours from the slightest hint of anything even faintly urban, there were no other cars on the road, and corn stretched as far as the eye could see. When we opened the car doors to let the kids romp on the grass between the Mickey D's and the surrounding palisades of corn, the only sounds we heard were buzzing insects and rustling corn stalks.

My wife went in first to use the bathroom while I stayed out with the kids and changed diapers. After diaper duty was done, my wife came back and I went in. The only other customers inside were two old ladies sitting drinking coffee.

They turned to me and one said: "Hey, you're pretty handy with a diaper."

I smiled.

"We were watching you out the window," the other said. "That was fast work. Efficient."

"I've learned," I told them. "Only bad things come from delay when you're in that situation. He who hesitates is lost."

They laughed, and they were still sitting there drinking coffee when I left. We said goodbye to each other and I went out to load up the kids. When everyone was back in the saddle, we hit the drive-through for our snack and set out once again on the *via de la corn*. It's a good thing we stopped when we did—there wasn't another place for hours. Yet, even there, in a dusty, forgotten corner of the vast McDonald's empire ("The sun never sets on McDonald's"), I met a couple of new people. Later, I had to wonder, how had I come to meet that pair of old ladies in the middle of nowhere? What strange paths led us all to converge at that place at that time?

It was like what a friend noted once about the secret life of books. My friend was in the Navy and found himself one night on a ship in the Indian Ocean. He couldn't sleep, so he went down to the Ward Room where a sort of informal lending library had developed. Books that made their way onto the ship but didn't depart again (or at least hadn't yet) ended up on a shelf that anyone was free to borrow from. My friend picked one out at random and opened it up. Inside the front cover was an inscription: "To Edmund, Bozeman, Montana, 1956." My friend was struck with wondering about the path of that book which had brought it to rest there, bobbing in the Indian Ocean on a Navy destroyer, some 50 years later. How many people had read that book? What hands had touched it? A book launched into the world takes on a life of its own. There's no telling where it will end up or how it will get there.

I realized from my encounter in *The World's Loneliest McDonald's* that we humans circulate in the same way. It's amazing all the contacts we each have every day with so many other people, ranging from good friends to total strangers passed on the street. And it's surprising the impact those contacts have—for good or ill. We are often influenced by people who don't even know they've touched our lives, in matters both prosaic (like that guy with a cool bike trailer I saw and told my wife about, and now we own one, too) and profound (like a child I saw in a wheelchair who made me realize how lucky my family and I really are).

You don't even have to see a person to be impacted by them. There's someone in one of the apartment buildings near us who plays the saxophone—really well. We have no idea who the person is, but we love to lay in bed at night with our windows open and listen to the music, letting ourselves be transported by the beautiful melodies drifting in on the gentle night breeze.

Then there are the things we read. An old saying goes: "We are most influenced by the people we meet, and often we meet those people for the first time in the books we read."

What's really amazing as a parent is to realize that our kids are going to be launched into the world, and take on a life of their own, just like that book my friend found floating in the middle of the Indian Ocean. And our children will become the people who meet and most influence others (whether in person, by audio, print or some as yet undreamt of new technology). Everyone wants to make a difference in the world, to make an impact, and there's no greater difference a person can make than as a parent—to the life of the children entrusted to their care, and through those little people we parent to more souls than we can really imagine.

Scripture tells us: "A great number of wise men is the safety of the world . . ." Wis 6, 24.

My Mom was a stay-at-home parent, and when people would ask her (frequently with a whiff of condescension): "What do *you* do?" Mom used to love answering: "I'm raising the leaders of tomorrow."

And she was right. Whether it's the public leaders we all see in positions of high media exposure, or the quiet leaders making a difference in a million little ways everyday in kitchens and cubicles around the world, tomorrow belongs to the Moms and Dads of today—perhaps most especially in raising the leaders of tomorrow's families, those who will parent the next generation launched into the world after we're gone. The Moms and Dads embarked on the odyssey of parenting are the one's making the future (both literally and figuratively), and shaping the world of tomorrow—and not just through their own actions, but also through how they raise their children, which will impact their children's children after them, in a cascading cataract of influence stretching far into the future.

So to all those future-making Moms and Dads out there: Even when the prevailing fashions of current opinion don't comprehend what it is that you do (to the point that some people actually have to ask you, because they just don't get it), or why it's so vital, or why anyone would sacrifice so much of themselves for another in the vocation of parenting, never lose sight of the importance of your work. We're all depending on you, even those who don't know it!

"Pursue personal excellence."

Anonymous

37.

The Sporting Life

Once when I was in London, I stopped on a street corner to buy a ticket for a double-decker bus tour. A 20-something young lady was selling the tickets, and upon hearing what she thought of as "my accent" (as a Midwestern American I don't think I have an accent, but to a Brit I guess I do), she asked me where I was from.

"Oh a small town in the United States," I told her. "You probably never heard of it: South Bend, Indiana."

"Oh sure," she said, "I love the Pacers! Reggie Miller's my favorite player, except for Jordan. Do you fancy sport?"

"Yeah," I said, surprised. "I like sports."

"How do you feel about Manchester united?" she asked.

"Well," I said, baffled but trying to be friendly, "I'm glad they were able to get together."

Then it was her turn to look baffled.

Those of you who know soccer (or "football," depending on where you're from), will understand my blunder. Manchester united, with a lower case "u," is a town with good community spirit. Manchester United, with a capital "U," is the name of a famous football club, likely to engender brawling with devotees of opposing teams.

The British and Americans remain two people divided by a common language.

But as this was my first trip "across the pond," and the first time I'd ever been outside the USA, I had no idea. Our family didn't travel much when we were kids. In fact, the first time I set foot on an airplane I was 27. I guess when you've got eight kids, the prospect of buying enough plane tickets to transport two basketball teams worth of family in order to traverse the friendly blue skies can be a little daunting. That's why God invented full sized vans. But it also meant that if a destination couldn't be reached by van, we weren't likely to go there.

Periodically my humble origins will rise up to smite me at odd moments. Like when I was talking food with a friend just returned from China. This friend was trying to describe the taste of a sea food dish she tried in Hong Kong, and was looking for a comparison I would understand.

"Have you had calamari?" she asked.

I had not.

"Hmm . . ." she puzzled. "What about eel?"

"I'm from Indiana," I told her. "If it's not corn, or it doesn't eat corn, I haven't had it."

I really shouldn't give my Hoosier homeland a bad rap. After all, Indiana gave the world Johnny Appleseed, Orville Redenbacher, Bobby Helms ("Jingle Bell Rock"), and even the television (sort of, Philo Farnsworth worked in Fort Wayne, Indiana for several years). I could go on, but I digress.

I was thinking about my cultural limitations recently after talking to a friend who's teaching his kids Latin. This friend is a professor and happens to be fluent in Latin. It's pretty neat for a father to teach his kids Latin, and it's interesting how the things that we fathers know can open up possibilities for our kids. I thought of my own father, and looking at my siblings, I can see how each of us kids acquired different interests from him. Several of my siblings are into construction and carpentry, several are adept at auto repairs. All of us are voracious readers, and several of us are into writing. A few are into art, we all play at least one musical instrument, and two of my sisters are scientists. Several of us have a deeply ingrained yen to see what's around the next bend in the road and travel whenever we can. And you can see the threads of all of these interests running right back to Dad. He's a real renaissance man, one of the rare breed of self-educated people who didn't go to college, but who also never stopped learning.

And doing. He always had a project going at home. It wasn't anything Dad ever said that got us hooked on various of his diverse passions. He never told us to read, never carped at us to do physics experiments. We would just see him engaged in his myriad endeavors, and his enthusiasm made us kids want to try our own hand at whatever Dad had going. Bless Mom's heart, she was a good sport about it all and never complained about a carburetor on her kitchen counter or the clunking of her pots and pans when they were turned into a make-shift drum kit. All that activity, all that doing, got us kids excited about doing things, too.

I don't know Latin, though, so the chances of me teaching Latin to my kids are pretty slim. It made think that there's a corollary to the phenomenon of our own interests and knowledge as fathers opening possibilities for our kids: the corollary is that our own *limitations* can also be limitations for our kids. If we never pursue an activity, if we know nothing about some subject, the chances of our kids delving into those unknown possibilities dwindles.

Partly, there is no avoiding this. There's an old saying: "You can do anything, but you can't do everything." There are only so many hours in the day, and as Aeneas told Hector, no man has been given all gifts.

But Jesus made it clear that we have to strive to develop ourselves and our gifts as best we can. In the parable of the talents, Mt 25, 14-30, Jesus tells how a man was going on a journey, and entrusted his possessions to three servants. Two of the servants used the talents entrusted to them to go out and trade, and they generated profits. The third, however, was afraid. So he took the talent entrusted to him and buried it in the ground. Upon returning, the servants who had profitably used their talents were rewarded, but the one who buried his talent was punished as a wicked and lazy servant.

As Jesus also told us: "You are the light of the world. A city set on a mountain cannot be hidden. Nor do they light a lamp and then put it under a bushel basket; it is set on a lampstand, where it gives light to all the house. Just so, your light must shine before others . . ." Mt 5, 14-16.

We fathers have to keep our own fires burning bright, so that all the world can see the light—beginning with those who have a front row seat on our lives: our children. That means continuing to develop ourselves, opening up new territory in our own minds and experience and souls. Amid all the wonder God created there's plenty to get excited about, more than we'll ever be able to exhaust in this life. So we can just pick one thing to work on, pursue it as best we can, and then when the time comes we can pick another and keep on moving, one step at a time.

I know what you're thinking: *When am I going to do that? I don't even get a chance to sleep at night, I'm just trying to survive, and you want to talk about self-improvement projects?!* I know, I know. Believe me, I know. I'm in that same place right now. Sometimes you can only muster enough energy just to keep the dream alive—and that's no small feat in and of itself. My sister gave me a great, practical suggestion on how to do that: get a magazine subscription. She's built several boats over the years, and when she was a Ph.D. student she had the opportunity to pursue a master's degree in yacht design as a sideline to her Ph.D. program—and the course of study would have been free for her, given her standing as a Ph.D. student at the university. She was excited about it, and got all signed up for the program and was ready to go, when *surprise!* Her first baby came along. With a dissertation to finish and a new baby to take care of, she had to shelve her dream of sail boat design for the time being. A few years ago I was visiting her at her house and saw a stack of *Wooden Boat* magazines.

"What are these for?" I asked. "Are you building boats again?"

"No," she answered. "But I've got a few magazine subscriptions. They're a good way to keep the dream alive."

She'll get back to it someday, and in the meantime, she keeps the interest percolating in her life in a way that's concrete and manageable within the context of the demands of raising young children. In the same way, I know that I'll get back to some of my passions again, even though for now they have to take a back seat for the kids.

The other thing to remember is that just because you can't do *everything* doesn't mean that you can't do *anything*. My sister may not be building boats right now, but she did get a couple of sea kayaks and she takes her kids out on kayaking excursions on the Great Lakes. For me, while the idea of learning Latin doesn't seem feasible at the moment, I'm trying to learn the Angelus. It's a wee bit more manageable: 12 lines, rather than a whole language. I also figured now is my best chance to get it down, since we live within earshot of a church that rings its bells at twelve noon and 6 p.m., the traditional hours for saying the Angelus (along with 6 a.m., but our neighborhood church doesn't ring its bells in the morning, which is probably prudent for maintaining positive community relations). It's actually beautiful to hear the bells ring and be reminded that it's time to stop and get my copy of the Angelus and take a few minutes to join the Church in prayer, along with thousands of others around the world in a tradition that goes back centuries.

So while we may not be able to do all the things we'd like right now, that's okay. The kids are job one right now. That's our primary, and most important, responsibility—by far. We have to concentrate on taking care of that job first. Then we can use whatever remaining resources of time, energy and treasure we can deploy to work around the margins of that main task to continue stoking our fires to burn a little more brightly. We don't have to do everything, just something, whatever we can manage during this season of our life. When we do, it's not just for us—it's also for our kids. We are called to be the light of the world, and that light starts shining at home.

"I am only one, but I am one. I cannot do everything, but I can do something. And I will not let what I cannot do interfere with what I can do."

Edward Everett Hale

The Angelus

From www.ewtn.com

Recite daily at 6 a.m., 12 noon, and 6 p.m.

V: The Angel of the Lord declared to Mary:
R: And she conceived of the Holy Spirit.

Hail Mary, full of grace, the Lord is with thee; blessed art thou among women and blessed is the fruit of thy womb, Jesus. Holy Mary, Mother of God, pray for us sinners, now and at the hour of our death. Amen.

V: Behold the handmaid of the Lord.
R: Be it done unto me according to Thy word.

Hail Mary . . .

V: And the Word was made Flesh (genuflect).
R: And dwelt among us.

Hail Mary . . .

V: Pray for us, O Holy Mother of God.
R: That we may be made worthy of the promises of Christ.

Let us pray:

Pour forth, we beseech Thee, O Lord, Thy grace into our hearts, that we, to whom the incarnation of Christ, Thy Son, was made known by the message of an angel, may by His Passion and Cross be brought to the glory of His Resurrection, through the same Christ Our Lord.

Amen.

Regina Caeli

From www.ewtn.com

Recited in place of the Angelus from Easter to Trinity Sunday

V: Queen of Heaven, rejoice, alleluia.
R: For He whom you did merit to bear, alleluia.
V: Has risen, as he said, alleluia.
R: Pray for us to God, alleluia.
V: Rejoice and be glad, O Virgin Mary, alleluia.
R: For the Lord has truly risen, alleluia.

Let us pray:

O God, Who gave joy to the world through the resurrection of Thy Son, our Lord Jesus Christ, grant we beseech Thee, that through the intercession of the Virgin Mary, His Mother, we may obtain the joys of everlasting life. Through the same Christ our Lord.

Amen.

38

September 29

Feast Day of Saints Michael, Gabriel, and Raphael, Archangels

Keeping Company with Saint Michael the Archangel

Our three year old daughter Liz was in the backseat of the car while my wife was driving. Mom made a wrong turn.

"Grrr," my wife grumbled, "wrong turn!"

From the backseat Liz's voice chimed up: "Recalculating!"

That made my wife crack-up.

But while Mom was laughing out loud, Liz didn't see the humor.

"That's what the GPS always says when you make a wrong turn," Liz said.

Which is true. For those who don't have a GPS, I should explain. A "GPS"—which stands for "Global Positioning System"—is a little electronic device, about the size of a standard men's folding-wallet, which displays maps and shows your location on the map (hence the "global positioning"), and gives you directions to wherever you want to go. You type in the address for your intended destination, or pick a spot from lists of sites arranged by category on the GPS menu screens (such as restaurants, gas stations, museums, etc.), and the GPS will get you there. It's a sort of talking, electronic pocket-map. The talking comes in handy when you're behind the wheel of a car. It's pretty hard to read a map while driving, so the GPS has a voice that gives you oral instructions, turn-by-turn, blow-by-blow, all the way. So the GPS will say, for example: "In 300 feet, turn right on Catalpa." Then, if you don't turn right on Catalpa, the GPS voice says (with some disdain): "Recalculating," and figures another route to get you to your intended Global Positioning destination.

For Liz, there is a natural correlation between "wrong turn" and "recalculating," because throughout the entire three years of her life she's been hearing the GPS say "recalculating" when Mom or Dad make a wrong turn. But to us, her parents, it's funny—because for us the GPS is still novel and we don't have the same natural association between "wrong turn" and "recalculating." In our minds, the GPS retains its mystique as a marvel of modern engineering, and "recalculating" is still something vaguely amazing and unexpected—especially when you hear it coming from your three year old. But in Liz's experience, "recalculating" is a commonplace, a given. She has never lived in a world without the GPS acting as our personal on-board navigator, ready to "recalculate" at a moment's notice, right in our very own car.

It reminded me of one of our friends in Minnesota who grew up in Seattle, but has raised all her kids in Minnesota. A few years back we had an unexpectedly mild winter, coupled with a late and long Lent, which meant that birds were chirping and flowers poking through black earth when Easter rolled around. Our friend took this for granted, but her kids were floored. "Can you believe it?" her kids asked. "We'll be hunting Easter eggs in grass instead of snow! I'll bet we'll find them all this year!" (When you hide Easter eggs in snow, you can expect to still be finding them well into Ordinary Time). In our friends mind, having grown up in Seattle, it was strange every year to pull on gloves and boots to hunt for Easter eggs, but for her kids it was green grass at Easter that was exotic.

Perceptions and assumptions change over time. The Gauls went to sleep one night thinking they were still speaking Latin, and that they'd been speaking Latin continuously in the hundreds of years since the withdrawal of Roman troops, only to wake up one morning and be greeted by Irish missionaries who informed them that the language they spoke had long since transformed itself from Latin into something new. The same thing happened in Spain, and even in Italy itself, giving rise to three new languages that were each mutually unintelligible. The Gauls called their new language French and immediately set about trying to ban McDonald's.

It's the reality of these kinds of changes, little in themselves but massive in accumulation, that makes it interesting to read the annual "Mindset List" from Beloit College. It's a quick

154

gauge for tracking some of the evolving inter-generational changes of perspective in our own era. The "Mindset List" says things like: *For the incoming freshmen the phrase "sounds like a broken record" carries no first-hand experience, since they have never seen a record player or heard a broken record.* I was fairly shocked to read an item on a list a few years ago that said something to the effect of: *The incoming freshmen were never alive during The Cold War, they were born after The Berlin Wall came down, and the Soviet Union has never existed during their lifetime.* It was strange to realize that such a central, defining feature of the world during most of my lifetime was for them ancient history, and probably seemed slightly unreal, with little relevance to their own lives. Like some of my Grandma's stories used to seem to me when she'd tell me about life during World War II. But over the years, I've come to appreciate Grandma's reminiscences more and more. People of my Grandma's generation, people like Saint John Paul the Great and Pope Benedict XVI, who lived through those terrible times and those terrible wars, have much to teach us. And it's never long before the last generation's experience passes beyond our reach forever.

We're all in danger of being subjugated to what Cicero called the "tyranny of the present." The power of the passing moment, with all its flash and pressing sense of insistency, can lure us into the temptation of thinking our own experiences are the *only* experiences. As Frank Sheed put it: "Many people today live in a suburb of reality. Now, there's nothing wrong with living in a suburb, so long as you don't think that your suburb is the whole metropolis."

In *Orthodoxy*, G. K. Chesterton advised the antidote of "the democracy of the dead"—looking to tradition, to those who have gone before us, to gain different perspectives on life and ultimate reality. C. S. Lewis advised the same thing, recommending that for every modern book you read, you should also read one old book. It was a way, Lewis said, "to keep the clean sea breeze of the centuries blowing through our minds," sweeping away at least a few of the assumptions of the current age, which have a tendency to settle thick like dust on our thoughts—or if we can't sweep them away, to at least ruffle them enough to help us recognize where they lie.

As Lewis wrote in his introduction to *Athanasius: On the Incarnation*:

> Every age has its own outlook. It is specially good at seeing certain truths and specially liable to make certain mistakes. We all, therefore, need the books that will correct the characteristic mistakes of our own period. And that means the old books. All contemporary writers share to some extent the contemporary outlook—even those, like myself, who seem most opposed to it. Nothing strikes me more when I read the controversies of past ages than the fact that both sides were usually assuming without question a good deal which we should now absolutely deny. They thought that they were as completely opposed as two sides could be, but in fact they were all the time secretly united—united with each other and against earlier and later ages— by a great mass of common assumptions.

I think the same principal applies to Catholic devotions. Devotions are windows into the faith that help put us in touch with different aspects of the faith, different aspects of a reality and a truth that's too large to take into our minds or hearts all at one go. Talking about doctrine in his book *Catholicism*, Father Barron wrote: "Newman said that a complex idea is equivalent to the sum total of its possible aspects. This means, he saw, that ideas are only really known across great stretches of space and time, with the gradual unfolding of their many dimensions and profiles." In *Episode 6: The Church* of his *Catholicism* video series, Father Barron explained further:

> John Henry Newman to me is very helpful here. He talks about the development of doctrine. Newman says, look, ideas exist not on the printed page. Ideas exist in the play of lively minds. If I take in an idea, I analyze it, I judge it, I compare it, I contrast it, I turn it around. I then throw it to somebody else. They do the same thing. They toss it

back to me, it's in this lively play that the full panoply of the idea unfolds. Newman said, a real idea is equivalent to the sum total of its possible aspects. Only when I've seen all the different angles and profiles of an idea do I really understand it.

Think of it in terms of a physical object. Like St. Peter's Basilica. Now, I've seen St. Peter's up close. It looks a certain way. I've seen it from all the way across the city of Rome. I've seen it even from an airplane. I've seen it from the Janiculum Hill. In each perspective it looks different, a different aspect appears.

Devotions from earlier times in Church history are another way to see our faith from a different vantage point, and learn something of facets of the faith which may be less in the forefront of thought and discourse in our own day. It's a way, borrowing from G. K. Chesterton's remarks about saints in *Orthodoxy*, to re-emphasis "whatever the world neglects, which is by no means always the same element in every age."

The Feast Day of Saints Michael, Gabriel, and Raphael on September 29 is a great opportunity to begin delving into some devotions that were important components of the faith for past generations. September 29 used to be the Feast day of just Saint Michael the Archangel, and it was called Michaelmas Day. Today the feast day, and sadly Saint Michael himself, are among those things that Chesterton noted "the world neglects . . ." In his poem *Lepanto*, Chesterton wrote:

Saint Michael's on his Mountain in the sea-roads of the north
(Don John of Austria is girt and going forth.)
Where the grey seas glitter and the sharp tides shift
And the sea-folk labour and the red sails lift.
He shakes his lance of iron and he claps his wings of stone;
The noise is gone through Normandy; the noise is gone alone;

157

And it often seems that St. Michael must go it alone these days. It was not always so. Great saints like Francis of Assisi made it a point to keep company with St. Michael. St. Francis went on pilgrimage to Mount Gargano, a site in Italy where St. Michael appeared. St. Francis prayed outside the cave of Michael's appearance, but would not enter. He deemed himself too unworthy. The shrine, which is still located at Mount Gargano, is one of only two basilicas in all the Church not dedicated by a Bishop, as it was consecrated by the presence of St. Michael himself (the other is the Church of the Nativity in the Holy Land, consecrated by Christ's presence). St. Francis celebrated Michaelmas every year and practiced a St. Michael's lent for 40 days before Michaelmas. In fact, St. Francis had fasted and prayed for 40 days in honor of St. Michael before he received the stigmata. Padre Pio also encouraged pilgrimage to Mount Gargano and dedication to St. Michael.

Mont Saint Michel, a great medieval monastery located on a tidal island off the coast of Normandy (and the site of Chesterton's St. Michael in the *Lepanto* poem), was another place St. Michael appeared and a great center of pilgrimage in the middle ages. Charlemagne dedicated his kingdom to St. Michael at Mont Saint Michel. There was also national devotion to St. Michael in England, where in 1114 King Ethelred declared three days of national fasting prior to Michaelmas.

Other pilgrimage sites to Saint Michael included St. Michael's Mount, an island off the coast of Cornwall where St. Michael appeared, Castel Sant'Angelo in Rome where St. Michael appeared and ended a plague that was devastating Rome, and in places like the Michaelion (now destroyed) which was located in part of present day Istanbul (and where St. Michael appeared to Emperor Constantine). Saint Michael also appeared in other places around the world, such as San Miguel del Milagro in Tlaxcala, Mexico.

One tradition holds that Saint Michael aided Saint Patrick in driving the snakes out of Ireland, appearing on Skellig Michael, a rocky islet off the coast of Ireland, to assist St. Patrick. St. Michael helped Saint Joan of Arc in her mission to save France. In 1696 St. Michael appeared at Bar Convent in the British city of York, where he drove away a mob that was attacking the hidden church there (the church was hidden since it was illegal to practice Catholicism in England at that time). Pope Leo XIII composed a prayer to St. Michael invoking his aid to defend the Church against the attacks that the Pope foresaw would be directed against it. Blessed John Henry Newman composed verse in honor of St. Michael. St. Francis de Sales recommended veneration of St. Michael.

And there are many more, great saints and holy people throughout the ages that drew much from their devotion to St. Michael. For those of us new to his veneration, there are many ways to begin St. Michael devotions. There is the St. Michael Chaplet, litanies to St. Michael, the famous St. Michael prayer of Pope Leo XIII, and books about St. Michael. A great place to start is the EWTN website, which has a lot of good, solidly orthodox materials to help (and with all the strange stuff about angels out there, it's good to have a source you know you can rely on for sound materials). EWTN has free resources on-line, and some good aids for purchase at very low prices, including books, booklets, prayer books, guides to help pray the St. Michael Chaplet (including CD's and DVD's of Mother Angelica praying the Chaplet), prayer beads for the Chaplet, statues, medals, etc.

There are free resources on-line in other places, too, including St. Michael litanies and other guides to the St. Michael Chaplet. There are also different novenas to St. Michael on-line, and you can say any prayer for nine consecutive days for a novena, including Pope Leo XIII's St. Michael Prayer. There is poetry honoring Saint Michael, such as Blessed John Henry Newman's *St. Michael*, or James Russell Lowel's *St. Michael the Weigher*, both available on-line. In his book *All About the Angels*, Father Paul O'Sullivan, O.P. recommended frequent repetition of the short prayer: "Glorious Saint Michael, Prince of the Heavenly Court, pray for us now and at the hour of our death." Father O'Sullivan also advised keeping a picture of St. Michael where you will often see it, and saying "Glorious Saint Michael, I love you," when you do. You can make special foods to honor St. Michael's feast day, and some great recipes can be found free on-line at www.catholiccuisine.blogspot.com and at www.fisheaters.com. You can read the Divine Office on St. Michael's feast day (and www.divineoffice.org includes not just the readings, but also songs and audio of the readings, it's a great way to pray with the Church). A devotion I've seen in our area that I always love is to visit a statue of a saint on his or her feast day, and bring something like flowers, a candle, prayer cards, or prayer beads, to place at the statue, and pray there to the saint. And of course one of the best things you can do is attend mass on St. Michael's feast day—and maybe you'll even be lucky enough to have a church dedicated to St. Michael the Archangel in your area that you can visit for his feast day mass.

If Saint Michael is a little lonely these days, there's no reason for it, and the neglect is our loss. There are many devotions available to us to keep company with this great helper, who has been called "The First Christian" and "The First Apostle," and whose desire is to bring us to Christ. His aid is available to us, we only need to ask. And St. Michael is only one of the three great Archangels honored on September 29—there are great devotions to the archangels Gabriel and Raphael as well! We just need to get started. If we can make some time for St. Michael and the other archangels, we can begin to explore another aspect of our faith, another way to come closer to Christ, and progress further on our own journey.

Saint Michael the Archangel, pray for us!

"Anything less than the will of God for your life will bore you."

Unattributed, quoted by Rachel Balducci in *Rock Star for Jesus* on Faith and Family Live!

St Michael Prayer of Pope Leo XIII

Taken from www.ewtn.com

PRAYER TO SAINT MICHAEL THE ARCHANGEL

St. Michael the Archangel, defend us in battle.
Be our defense against the wickedness and snares of the
Devil.
May God rebuke him, we humbly pray,
and do thou, O Prince of the heavenly hosts,
by the power of God,
thrust into hell Satan,
and all the evil spirits, who prowl about the world
seeking the ruin of souls.
Amen.

"Pay no attention to the affairs of others, whether they be good or
bad, for besides the danger of sin, this is a cause of distractions and
lack of spirit."

St. John of the Cross

39

Theology Lessons From a Two Year Old

Human beings have a desire to impose order on the universe. But much like a parent's desire to impose order on their kids' toys, it often goes unsatisfied. With the toys, at least we have a fighting chance (depending on the age of the kids and the volume of plastic flowing in from grandparents—and what is it about toys with innumerable little pieces and parts that delight grandparents so?). Not so with the universe. It's got way too many pieces and parts, and it's way too big—and we're just too small.

I had an interesting experience watching a movie with my oldest daughter who's two and a half. We were watching an animated Disney movie. It seems that animated movies are all we watch these days, and a prerequisite for any video entertainment in our household is the presence of talking animals. Its funny how times change. In college we spoke in a code comprised of lines borrowed from *Seinfeld* and *Cheers*. Now I find my conversations peppered with references to movies like *Ratatouille* and *Winnie the Pooh*. If an intellectual concept can't be conveyed in analogies drawn from the pre-school canon, I doubt my ability to communicate it.

Anyway, there we were watching our animated movie, and though it had the required talking animals, it was just a bit too advanced for my daughter's two-year-old brain. She couldn't follow the plot, grasp who the characters were, or understand their relationships to each other. What was interesting, though, was that she satisfied her need to draw order out of the chaos by imposing a meaning of her own devising on everything she saw and heard. As we watched the movie together, she re-narrated the whole thing, making up her own story that incorporated all the elements present in the movie, but fitting them together in a new way that had nothing to do with the actual movie. She even re-named the characters with her own identifiers (such as "the red lady" and "the little mouse").

Her re-configured story emerged in real time, blow-by-blow as we watched the movie. "So there the red lady is talking to the little girl, and she's wondering if the little girl wants to do a craft," she'd say, when in actuality the "red lady" was the villain of the movie and was conniving against the "little girl," who was the heroine and victim. Then the movie cut to the next scene and we'd see one of the talking mice. "And there is the little mouse," Liz noted. "He's going to do a craft with the little girl and the red lady," when actually the "little mouse" was trying to rescue the "little girl." And so it went throughout the whole movie. Later that night our daughter was still working it all over in her head, refining, embellishing, and explaining it to me as I put her to bed.

I was reminded of a story related by Father Robert Barron in *Catholicism*, the companion book to his wonderful *Catholicism* video series, about "William James and his dog":

> In an essay toward the end of his life, the great American philosopher told of his dog, who would typically enter his master's office at the end of the workday to receive a pat on the head. The animal, James explained, would look around the cluttered room and see the thousands of books on the shelves, the many papers covering the desk, and the globe that rested in the corner. He would see them but understand them hardly at all. And if James made bold to expatiate on the meaning of these things – that the books were collections of symbols evocative of ideas, that the papers, by a similar semiotic system, conveyed intelligent messages, that the globe was a representation of the spherical planet that both master and dog inhabited – the animal would have looked at him with utter incomprehension. But then it occurred to James that we are in a similar relation to a higher mind. Is it possible that we, like the dog, see everything there is to see, but actually *understand* it in only the most superficial way? And is it the case that the higher

163

intelligence could not, even in principle, begin to explain the deepest meaning of things to us, due to the limited capacity of our minds?

Maybe the main difference between humans and dogs is that we bipeds are more prone to what Hilaire Belloc, in *The Path to Rome*, called (in a classic Bellocism), "*intellectual pride*, than which no sin is more offensive to the angels." We think we know more than we do.

As Scripture tells us: "What exists is far-reaching; it is deep, very deep: who can find it out?" Eccl 7, 24. "How weighty are your designs, O God; how vast the sum of them!" Ps 139, 17. "Beyond these, many things lie hid; only a few of His works have we seen." Sir 43, 34.

It's in our Egypt moments especially that we need to remember that "He does great things beyond our knowing; wonders past our searching out." Job 37, 5. There are times when God calls us to arise and venture forth on a great journey, but all we can see from where we sit in our own little Egypt is the Red Sea blocking our way ahead, Pharaoh in hot pursuit behind, and beyond a desert full of thirst and starvation. To us, God's call can seem nonsensical, difficult in the extreme, even frightening. That's when we need to keep in mind that we "know not the work of God which He is accomplishing in the universe." Eccl 11, 5.

C. S. Lewis wrote of our condition in *The Horse and His Boy*. The boy in the story is named Shasta and he is lost in the mountains, trying to make his way through to Narnia:

> He had never been in mountain country before . . .
> the sun was getting ready to set . . . Then they
> plunged into the fog, or else the fog rolled over
> them. The world became gray. Shasta had not
> realized how cold and wet the inside of a cloud
> would be; nor how dark. The gray turned to black
> with alarming speed . . . he could see nothing at all.
> * * * * * [And then he had] a sudden fright. Shasta
> discovered that someone or something was walking
> beside him. It was pitch dark and he could see
> nothing. And the Thing (or Person) was going so

quietly that he could hardly hear any footfalls. What he could hear was breathing. His invisible companion seemed to breath on a very large scale . . .

The invisible companion turns out to be none other than Aslan himself. Shasta makes it through the mountains and the next day, after the sun rose, he "turned and looked behind him . . . 'I see,' Shasta said to himself . . . 'I must have come through the pass in the night. What luck that I hit it! – at least it wasn't luck at all really, it was *Him*."

That's the situation we are all in: traveling through a thick fog, at night, in unfamiliar country, trying to make our way home. And it's good to know that, like Shasta, we're not alone. The large scale but invisible *He* is with us, and He will keep us on track and lead us to safety, if we will heed His direction. It was our Mother Mary, in her last words recorded in the Gospel, who told us at Cana how to find our way: "Do whatever He tells you." Jn 2, 6.

And the funny thing is that, even with our limited understanding, if we do choose to follow Him in our blindness, we can come to see. For as Scripture also promises: "Those who trust in Him shall understand truth . . ." Wis 3, 9.

"He is no fool, who gives what he cannot keep to gain what he cannot lose."

Jim Elliot

40.

Blessed Newman and the Sailor

Do you ever stop and wonder at the different paths that people take in life? Sometimes I think about the other kids on my block from when I was growing-up. Most have "normal" lives like mine—it was school, a job, marriage, family, and they still live in the same town we grew-up in. One family was a little different. They didn't own a car when we were growing-up. They walked or rode bikes everywhere. They had a son my age, and we were pretty good friends. He ended up going to a top-drawer college, lived abroad in Germany and Russia, and then landed a job on Wall Street. He rode his bike over the Brooklyn Bridge everyday on his way to work at the New York Stock Exchange. Then he got some big ticket graduate degrees in business. Now he's a high-powered executive—at Ford Motor Company. He makes cars for a living! Go figure.

An even more surprising transformation happened with one of my friends from college. He was from the "corn belt" like me, and had never travelled more than a hundred miles from his home. But in college he joined the Navy ROTC program. The first time he ever saw the ocean was when he reported for duty on his first ship. Well, it turned out he had salt water in his veins all along: he loved the ocean, he loved sailing, he loved the Navy, and the Navy loved him. He was a natural, particularly at "ship driving." Whenever his ship got in tight quarters, the Captain put him at the helm. He continued to rise up through the ranks long after his ROTC buddies had mustered out and gone back to dry land for desk jobs or grad school.

We got together a few years back, and he told me a story about returning to port once after a six month stint at sea. He was standing on the deck of his ship early in the morning when a seaman came up to him.

"We should get back to port tomorrow," the seaman said. "Are you excited, Sir?"

"Excited?" my friend answered. "That's always one of the saddest days for me, to see a thoroughbred like this ship hobbled to a pier. Sailors belong on ships, and ships belong at sea."

The seaman was a little surprised. Like all offices, even those that float, complaining about work was a staple of idle conversation.

"When I die," my friend added, "I want my ashes mixed with a can of Davy's Gray and painted on the side of a ship. That way I'll always be at sea."

It struck me as a good way to approach life's work. Not aiming to scrape by with the barest minimum possible, waiting for all the headaches and hassles to pass and finally be over, but instead embracing life and our vocation in it with zeal, eager for the adventure. Scripture tells us:

> . . . all men are of clay,
> for from earth man was formed;
> Yet with His great knowledge the Lord makes men unlike;
> in different paths He has them walk.
>   * * *
> Like clay in the hands of a potter,
> to be molded according to His pleasure,
> So are men in the hands of their Creator,
> to be assigned by Him their function.
> Sirach 33, 10-13

We were made to do some work for God—probably many works for God—and it's good to remember that we're pilgrims *on a mission* in this world. Cardinal John Henry Newman, now Blessed Newman, composed a prayer I first ran across hanging on the wall of a humble home of an old miner and carpenter, who had also been in the Navy as a Marine in World War I. Newman's prayer reads:

God has created me
to do Him some definite service.
He has committed some work to me
which He has not committed to another.
I have my mission.
I may not know what it is in this life.
But I shall be told in the next.
I am a link in a chain,
a bond of connection between persons.
He has not created me for nothing.
I shall do good. I shall do His work.
Therefore I will trust Him.
Whatever I do, wherever I am, I cannot be thrown away.
If I am in sickness, my sickness may serve Him.
If I am in sorrow, my sorrow may serve Him.
He does nothing in vain. He knows what He is about.

When Blessed Newman was beatified, his intellectual legacy, his writing, scholarship, erudition, and contributions to theology, were all widely celebrated. And rightly so. But in addition to these, I think of Blessed Newman also as a patron for the common man, reminding us that we are all links bound together in a common chain. Miners and marines, sailors and saints. We all have something we share: a mission given to us by God. The transformations that happen as we pursue the adventure of that mission can be surprising. Like the corn-belt kid turned sailor. And I'd guess when Blessed Newman started out as an Anglican preacher he never expected to end up as a cardinal in the Catholic Church. But even though we don't know where our mission may take us, perhaps far from where we began, or what may happen along the way—and even when we don't know exactly *what* the work is which God has given us—we're doing it every day. Just as Blessed Newman had his work, we each have our work that we, and we alone, are to do—and it's set before us each morning. Much in the world would divide us and seek to hobble us, tying us to a pier when what we really need is to brave the storms and put out into the deep. Blessed Newman's prayer can be a great daily reminder that we are pilgrims on a mission, and we can pray to him to help us accomplish the tasks which would go undone without us.

"Joy is the noblest human act."

St. Thomas Aquinas

41.

A Point of Reference

Many years ago, when I was a young man (or as I prefer to think of it, a *younger* man), I went on a long Western road trip one summer with a college buddy. We drove 9,000 miles in two weeks. Of all that windshield time, what I remember most is Montana. We got to understand why they call it Big Sky Country. East of the Little Big Horn Mountains (and most of Montana is east of the mountains), the country is flat and unbroken as far as the eye can see.

All that grows there is long, waving grass.

There is nothing to break up the view.

It's just sky.

Enormous, endless sky, mile after empty mile.

My friend was driving and I was looking out the window.

"This landscape can really mess with your perception," he said, breaking me from my reverie.

"Uh-huh," I agreed.

"Try to pick out something," he said, gesturing out into the emptiness ahead of us, "and see how long it takes us to get to it."

I searched the horizon and tried to find some differentiating feature I could use for a landmark.

I thought I saw a telephone pole in the distance.

"Ok," I said, "I've got something."

"That telephone pole?" he asked.

"Yeah," I said.

"That's what I figured," he said. "It's the only thing out there. Ok, now watch it."

I watched the pole.

Slowly, slowly, very slowly, we drew closer to it.

"Now," he asked, "how fast do you think we're going?"

"65?" I speculated.

"Faster."

"75?"

"Faster."

170

"85?"

"Faster, a lot faster."

"How fast are we going?" I asked, getting a little nervous.

"95."

"WHAT!?!"

"Yeah," he said. "The speed just creeps up on you. Doesn't feel like we're going that fast, does it? It's weird. With no point of reference, you really can't tell."

I had a similar experience recently with our daughter. Not that she's driving—she's only six months old right now, so driving isn't an issue yet. But sleeping is an issue. A big one. Actually, lots of little, practical details are issues at this stage: bottles, eating solids, diapers.

We're learning to take things one day at a time. Sometimes she demands a bottle. Sometimes she won't take a bottle. Sometimes she'll eat solids—and she makes a prodigious mess when she does. Sometimes she won't eat solids—and she makes a prodigious mess flinging rejected baby food across the room.

More than anything, though, we've been surprised at how everything takes so much time. We used to get our chores done quick and spend most of our weekends outdoors: riding bikes, going to the beach, hiking, visiting with friends. Now it seems like a major accomplishment just to get the laundry done. So many hours go into rocking our daughter to sleep, feeding her, changing her, dressing her, etc., you wonder if it will ever end, and you start to forget what life was like B.C. ("Before Children").

I was talking to one of my brothers on the phone recently. He has a son who just turned three, and my brother was telling me about taking his son fishing for the first time.

"That sounds like a lot of fun," I told him.

"Oh yeah," my brother agreed. "It's great when you can start doing stuff like that with them. I just can't believe how quick they grow up."

"I just wish we could get Liz to sleep," I said.

"Still waking up a lot at night?" he asked.

"Yeah, two or three times."

"Does she need to be rocked back to sleep?" he asked.

"Yeah, and it takes forever."

"I'll tell you what to do," he said. "Watch the clock. The clock will be your best friend. I know it feels like its endless when you're walking her at night, but watch the clock and you'll be amazed at how fast it really goes."

I took his advice.

He was right!

At three in the morning, it feels like endless hours as you walk back and forth in the baby's room. You think you must be putting a thousand miles of tread on ten feet worth of carpet. But when I watched the clock, I was amazed: in reality, it only took six minutes to get her back to sleep.

All I needed was a point of reference to put things in perspective.

In the short run, the clock is a great point of reference. But for the big work of parenting, God gave us the real reference point to put our task into perspective: eternity.

God "put eternity into man's mind . . ." Eccl 3, 11. As John told us, "you have eternal life." 1 Jn 5, 13. Jesus said of his followers, "I give them eternal life, and they shall never perish . . ." Jn 10, 28. "[T]he free gift of God is eternal life in Christ Jesus our Lord." Rom 6, 23.

We're going to live forever, *and our kids are too*. So when it gets hard, remember the magnitude of our calling as parents: "an eternal weight of glory beyond all comparison . . ." 2 Cor 4, 17, and know that it's worth the effort. Everything we put into our parenting now will endure—forever.

Plus, it's good to know that our kids will have plenty of chances to pay us back for those 3 a.m. feedings. And remember that this too shall pass—probably a lot quicker than we realize. When your brother tells you that he's taking his son fishing, and you remember that son being born (what was it, just yesterday?), suddenly you realize that we fathers really are barreling down the highway at 95 miles an hour, even if we can't feel the speed. As St. Paul tells us: "Fight the good fight of the faith; take hold of the eternal life to which you were called . . ." 1 Tm 6, 12.

42.

What's a Baby Cost?

When my wife and I found out we were having our first baby, I was ecstatic. The coming of the new baby filled all my thoughts. I got to be a boring conversationalist, with only one topic to discuss. It was uncanny the connections I now saw (which had never been apparent to me before) between every conceivable subject and babies. And not just babies generically, but our new baby in particular. An unsuspecting friend might innocently ask: "How's the weather?" And I'd answer: "Well, our baby is due in February, so I hope we won't have to worry about snow when it's time to get to the hospital."

I was a direct-TV dish pointed at only one light in the sky: the baby satellite. That was the only channel playing in our house, and it was on 24/7: all baby, all the time. Amid the frenzy of baby-mania, we felt the urge to *do something*, to prepare in some way. A new baby was coming, so what should we do? How should we get ready?

One of our friends who already had kids suggested ominously: "Get as much as sleep as you can."

At the time, we didn't understand what she meant. We've learned since. That was good advice.

But when you're in the grip of baby-fever, you can't sleep. You want to be doing *something*. Anything. Vast commercial empires are built on this compulsive anxiety of expectant parents, and we rendered unto many of them. We bought things, amassing a small library of baby literature. We packed. Our hospital bag was sitting by the front door months before the due date, complete with alternate coming-home-from-the-hospital outfits to handle either contingency: boy or girl. We made plans, including creating a new budget in anticipation of diapers and formula. But, we worried, what other baby related expenses might we be missing? Were we overlooking some indispensable baby-gadget the existence of which we neophyte parents were as yet unaware?

To be sure no stone was left unturned, I called one of my brothers who already had kids and asked him: "What's a baby cost?"

He gave us another ominous answer.

"As much as you've got," he said.

Gulp.

That wasn't exactly the response I was looking for.

Into the surprised silence emanating from my end of the telephone line he elaborated:

"Look," he said, "you can spend as much or as little as you want on a baby. Take cribs. We needed a crib, so we started shopping around. You can get one for $60 at Wal-Mart, or you can buy one custom-made for $4,000 at a baby boutique. One place we checked-out you had to call in advance and get an appointment to even look at their stuff. Now, do you need a $4,000 crib? Well, there are people who think so, and if you listen to them you'll start thinking you need one too. But there's people from every point of the economic spectrum having kids, and I guaranty you they don't all have $4,000 cribs. You spend what you've got. If you have more, you'll spend more—and you'll think you need more. But if you have less, you'll spend less and you'll need less. You find other ways to do things besides money."

All the cryptic advice from family and friends, mixed with the confusion from the baby books (all of which were quite authoritative on matters of baby care, and many of which contradicted each other), created a disorienting mess. It was like the swirl of indistinct colors projected on a cathedral floor from a stained glass window high overhead: a pool of hazy hues, a color-soup with splashes of red and blue and green all faded and indistinct at the edges and jumbled together, in which no coherent design can be discerned.

The empires of infant-advice dispensers had built a *Tower of Baby* fit to rival the *Tower of Babel*—with the same confusing result. Either you had to let babies cry it out, or do attachment parenting. Breast feed until age one (some insisted on two and some say even later), or start solids at 4 months. Many an old grandmother advised me to add a little rice to a baby's bottle at bed-time to help them sleep through the night. Others wouldn't dream of feeding their kids anything that wasn't 100 % organic, all-natural, and hand-pureed by themselves. There are debates about cloth diapers versus disposable diapers (and then debates about the attributes of various brands of disposable diapers). And there's even a new movement advocating no diapers at all. Don't laugh. You may not have heard of this emerging trend, and you may think it sounds like a devious plot hatched by manufacturers of tile flooring to increase the need and demand for their easily-mopped products, but before you cast stones at those living in linoleum houses, I'll tell you I know people who adhere to this new no-diaper-paradigm and they swear by it. Imagine children potty trained by 9 months. They say it can happen. I've never experienced such a thing myself, but I sure wish I had!

Into the maelstrom of competing theories, Scripture sheds some much needed light. The Bible tells us: "As one faces differs from another, so does one human heart from another." Prv 27, 19.

It's funny to look back now on our thoughts about what parenting would be like before we had kids. We were hung-up and stressed out about a lot of minutia that turned out to be ancillary. There's a saying that what seems urgent is rarely truly important, and what is truly important rarely seems urgent. Strollers and basinets and all the rest of the ever multiplying paraphernalia of infant care can seem urgent. You feel like you have to get that white-noise generator pronto. But what's really important, and what rarely comes up in the baby-books or classes, is love.

We're all different people, we're all different parents, and we all do things in different ways—which is probably just as it should be, because each child we parent is unique, too. The color-soup projected on the cathedral floor from the stained glass window overhead may not present any discernable design, but lift your eyes to the window above and you can see how the different pieces fit together. At least, as long as the sun is shining through them. Without the sun, there's no image at all—no light, no color. Just a mass of dark and dull leaded-glass. The real soul of a stained glass window isn't in the bits of glass, it's in the sun that shines through and illumines each. And it's the same sun for all, different as each of the individual pieces of glass may be.

What's really important in parenting is to let the light of love shine through us as we care for our kids, with or without diapers, in "some assembly required" cribs or custom-crafted heirloom cradles. When that light shines, it's a beautiful thing to see all the different bits of glass glowing, each in its own color. And best of all is to see our own kids shining with that same light.

"Sin has many tools, but a lie is the handle which fits them all."

Oliver Wendell Holmes

43

Halloween

Over the years of my childhood, I experienced a transformation of Halloween. When I was young, we donned costumes and wandered the neighborhood with Dad trick-or-treating, and always had a good time. Mom's seamstress skills and ninja-mad crafting capabilities helped create some fantastic Halloween-night ensembles. She sewed Dracula capes and fuzzy Daniel Boone coon-skin caps. And Mom had a dash of sparkling, masquerade-manufactory genius coursing through her veins. She always came up with the extra little touches that turned a costume into a memory. Like the year I dressed as a hobo. I wore one of Dad's suit vests, a tie, an old fishing cap, and tied a red bandana to the end of a stick that I carried over my shoulder. Then came that special Momma flourish: she smeared a little Crisco along my jaw and pressed coffee grounds into it, and voila! I had a beautiful hobo stubble. In a stroke, with that one little bit of costuming magic, I was transformed from just another Halloween bum into the King of the Road.

And one year Mom made a legend by creating a costume like no other: a lion suit that still stands amid the annals of Halloween as the greatest work of the costuming art ever conceived and executed outside a *Star Wars* film set. The body was sewn from golden-brown faux-fur material. She knit a lion's tail and sewed it to the furry lion suit. All very nice, but what really brought the *wow* was the mane. Mom knit a head piece that you pulled on like a hat, except it covered your whole head and neck, leaving only your face open. Then she fastened (whether by crocheting, hooking, or tying, I don't know) hundreds of strands of yarn—brown, red, gold, and orange—all over the headpiece, creating a luxuriant, shaggy mass of radiant lion mane—and there were even two neat, little, knit lion ears protruding from the dense profusion of waving mane. To finish it off, Mom knit lion paws and feet that you pulled on like mittens and socks, adorned with the same glorious yarn-shag as the mane. It was *awesome*—and it's still in use to this day, some 30 years later, now by Mom's grandkids.

Other people's costumes could be as much fun as our own. We took turns manning the candy distribution center at our own homestead, and passing out candy was the best way to see the fanciful fabrications from the fertile imaginations of our fellow Halloween revelers. Dad would take the top panel off our storm door, and we would sit inside the door on a stool, handing out candy through the open panel, exchanging "Trick-or-Treats!" and "Happy Halloweens!" with other merry-makers. I remember a pair of kids that were dressed as a set of fuzzy dice, in boxes painted red with white dots on them. And there were the Christmas presents: kids wearing boxes covered with wrapping paper, ribbon and bows. Tinfoil knights, hairy werewolves, and green faced Frankenstein's all passed by our door. One of my favorites was a family with all the kids dressed as playing cards. They wore panels of cardboard on front and back attached together by ropes that hung on the shoulder, like the old-fashioned sandwich board signs you see people wearing in photos from the 40's. The back panel was painted like the back of a playing card, the front like the face of the card. I was too young to recognize card hands at the time, but I wonder if they made a full house all together?

And of course leading up to the big night we'd have already made our annual trek to the pumpkin patch and carved our pumpkins with triangle eyes and nose and a square-toothed jack-o-lantern grin. Then we'd light candles inside their hollowed out shells and watch them glow orange in the dark. We made felt witches, ghosts, and pumpkins that we hung on our walls and windows, and a scarecrow stuffed with leaves to stand guard on our front steps. We enjoyed our Halloweens, and we knew how to celebrate them right.

But there was no mistaking the change that was underway with Halloween, even then, and one year Mom and Dad finally made the decision that our family would do something different. They instituted a Harvest Festival for our family. We still went to the pumpkin patch, and carved our pumpkins, and made our scarecrow, and all our felt crafts. But instead of costumes and trick-or-treating, we did Harvest games and had treats at home. The games were things like bobbing for apples, pin the nose on the pumpkin, sack races, and a clothes pin drop. We carried bags that got filled with treats and surprises at each of the different game stations: candy, spider rings, glow wands and other items of delight and deliciousness. The crown of the evening came at the very end, when, tired and satiated and filled with fun, we all lay down on the floor in our living room in front of a crackling fire. Mom and Dad turned all the lights off, and read spooky stories to us by the firelight. The long, wavering shadows cast by the flickering flames added to the eerie thrill of it all. It must not have been *too* scary, though, as testified to by the number of little ones who had to be carried to their beds when the stories were over. The Harvest Festivals were every bit as much fun as the trick-or-treating had been.

Now that I have kids of my own, I like the idea of Harvest Festivals even more. The downward spiral of Halloween has continued over the ensuing years. For one, a lot of Halloween just isn't that much fun anymore. In the last few years, we've had kids come to our door with only the barest pretense of a costume—and some no costume at all. I've passed out candy to kids and gotten nary a "Thank you!" or "Happy Halloween!" in return. Instead, I've actually had kids hold their bags out to me again and demand: "Give me more." After one of those responses, I looked over at the kid's parents. But the parents weren't the least bit phased or put out. They just stood there, staring sullenly at me, with an expression that seemed to say: *You heard her, fork over the candy.* That kind of Halloween experience doesn't seem very festive. Just greedy. It's more like looting the local Wal-Mart after a natural disaster and calling it a community celebration.

Then there are those who don't really qualify as kids anymore and should have retired their nights of trick-or-treating some years ago.

Mostly, though, there is an unmistakable darkness to the new Halloween. A darkness that didn't used to be there, and which seems to be growing.

It's unfortunate, because as much as I enjoyed our Harvest Festivals as a kid, I also loved our Halloweens when we were still trick-or-treating, and I wish my kids could have that kind of experience, too. But wishing won't make it so, and Halloween just isn't what it was then. So, as a parent, you do what you can—where you are, with what you've got. "Bloom Where You Are Planted," as my Mom embroidered in one her needlework "Threads of Wisdom" sayings that hung around our house when I was growing up. Which, really, is particularly appropriate for celebrating the vigil of a feast honoring all saints.

Because that's just what the saints did: the best they could, in answering God's call and doing God's will, right now: where they were, in the times they found themselves living in. And you can be sure those times were never perfect, that all temptation and violence and greed and corruption and all the rest of the baggage of a fallen world was never banished. No, the saints lived in a world of sin and death, just like you and I do, and they acted amidst circumstances that ranged from difficult, at best, to downright tortuous and deadly at worst.

There's a temptation we all face to get sidetracked in our own imaginings of how we *think* we'd like the world to be, both for our own personal good and that of the greater cosmos at large. But in *The Secret Knowledge*, a book that's about contemporary politics on one level, but human cosmology on another, David Mamet says: "The question 'What would you do differently?' . . . is not only a foolish but a costly indulgence. The useful question is, 'What will you do *now*?'"

Mother Teresa expressed something similar when she said: "Yesterday is gone. Tomorrow has not yet come. We have only today. Let us begin."

We can only act in the here and now, doing the best we can where and when we are. But we can take some confidence in remembering, as Blessed John Henry Newman wrote in one of his prayers: "God has created me to do Him some definite service . . . He does nothing in vain. He knows what He is about." We may not understand our own messy, chaotic, corrupt, dark, frustrating, and often maddening times, but God chose us for *this* moment, in *this* place. And He knows what He is about. One little step we can take is to find a way, as best we can, to keep the feast and vigil of All Hallows Day as it should be kept. After all, the saints who have gone before us have won the crown of sainthood, and that is something worth celebrating. And they are praying for us and helping us right now, and that's worth celebrating, too.

These days will pass away, but the saints will remain—we have much to be thankful for!

"The Lord is at hand. Have no anxiety about anything, but in everything by prayer and supplication with thanksgiving let your requests be made known to God. And the peace of God, which passes all understanding, will keep your hearts and your minds in Christ Jesus."

Saint Paul, Philippians 4, 5-7

44

Hard Traveling

My Mom and Dad are exactly the sort of people you'd love to go on a road trip with. If you happen to be a Benedictine monk.

Just kidding, of course. Even Benedictines find Mom and Dad a little austere.

Most notorious of their ascetic proclivities is the (in)famous "iron-bladder" straight-through policy. If a trip can be made in 10 hours or less, don't expect any pit-stops with Mom or Dad at the helm. Be prepared for the long haul once you settle yourself into the well-worn bucket seats set deep within the ponderous, huge hunk of metal that is now a Johnny-Cash-esque 1965, '66, '67, '68, '69, Dodge-Chevy-Ford truck as a result of Dad's constant patching together of various mechanical oddments to keep his pick-up running. Dad's truck is the junk-yard equivalent of the Island of Unwanted Toys in the old *Rudolph the Red-Nosed Reindeer* clay-mation holiday special. All the lonely and abandoned alternators and transmissions and axles and other pieces and parts from forgotten wrecks were collected together by Dad to create a—shall we say "unique"—Frankenstein of the road.

Only the hardy need apply for passage. Once the key turns in the ignition, the doors are hermetically sealed. There's no stopping, exiting, or pulling over to grab a quick bite until the final destination is reached. You're only succor or solace once you pull away from the curb with Mom and Dad is prayer.

Really.

They pray a lot. Especially on road trips. They always bring their rosary beads and praying the rosary is one of their favorite traveling activities. I join in when I'm along with them, though I do have to admit that on occasion I may have prayed to run low on gas just so Dad would be compelled to stop somewhere.

So it was with some trepidation, on a fine morning one day in early autumn, that I approached a road trip with Mom and Dad to visit one of my brothers in a far flung locale so remote from our Midwestern home that it bordered a salt sea on something called "the coast." It was a twelve hour trek—very important, as it meant that we would get one precious, if brief, stop somewhere around the half-way mark. Other than that, it would be six hours of solid and uninterrupted windshield time on either side of the break.

Dad was driving, I was navigating and sat up front in the passenger seat, and Mom had the bench seat behind us all to herself. Things started well enough. We said a rosary first thing, then listened to some music.

"It's a little warm back here," Mom called out.

Dad adjusted the air-conditioner, turning the temperature down and the blower-fan up.

We continued driving and talking. Mom chirped up again from the back seat: "Could we have a little more AC please?"

Dad dutifully turned the AC temperature setting down and the blower up. I re-adjusted myself to get my knees away from the air vent. It was getting pretty cold.

"A little colder please," Mom called again.

Dad didn't question Mom, he just turned the AC even lower.

This continued every 10 minutes or so, with Mom asking: "Could we have a little more AC?" or "It's a little warm back here" or simply "a little cooler please," and Dad adjusting the temperature down with each request.

Now, you have to understand that, much like Han Solo said of the *Millennium Falcon* in *Star Wars*, Dad's truck has a lot of "special modifications." He's never content simply to fix something. He operates according to the "Holy Spirit Principle"— if you're going to touch something, don't just leave like it was. Juice it up. Make it better and bolder than before. And over the years Dad has fiddled with just about every component of his truck, so it's all been revved-up real good by now. Like his air-conditioning. It's no longer your standard automobile AC unit. I think Dad rigged-up an old, salvaged refrigerator to run on diesel. And his blower fan may once have been a single-prop airplane engine in a former life that he somehow managed to finagle into place under the hood. That's the kind of serious power Dad imparts to his machines, and with Mom continuing to call for "a little more

AC please," "a little cooler please," we ended up driving in an ice-box with Dad's over-muscled AC set-on "sub-arctic" and the blower fan producing a hurricane force gale.

Now I was praying for Mom and Dad to start another rosary just to distract Mom from asking for more cold.

My breath was frosting in front of my face. Dad's nose was running. I had to scrape ice off the *inside* of the windshield. After hours of enduring this man-made meteorological phenomenon, Dad finally asked: "Are we re-re-ready for a br-br-break?"

I nodded my head.

"Is that a yes, or are you just shivering?" Dad asked.

"That's a ye-ye-yes," I chattered.

"Sounds good," Mom said from the back seat, completely impervious to the blizzard created in the truck cab at her behest.

When we finally stopped, I looked back at her while trying to straighten my frozen joints to get out of the truck. It took me a second to spot her. Mom had disappeared within a fuzzy mass of yarn that seemed to have exploded all over the backseat of the truck. She was completed covered from head to toe with heaps of wool wound into brightly colored strands. She'd been using the time on the road to work on some sort of monumental knitting project—from the looks of it she was fulfilling a special order to outfit the Russian army with pastel colored afghans for winter. All you could see of her was a smiling face and two knitting needles protruding from an Everest sized mountain of wool. A thousand bleating quadrupeds must have yielded-up their fleeces to produce the bales of yarn Mom was hidden beneath. For an instant I saw in my minds' eye a vast flock of frigid sheep, naked and shorn, shivering on a windswept hill somewhere in Ireland. I could feel their pain. I pitied them (and myself) for the icy agony of it all.

"No wonder you're warm!" I told her. "We're freezing up here while you're wrapped in a cocoon of wool!"

"Oh Jacob," she said. "I'm knitting blankets for the grandkids. Why don't you just drink a cup of hot coffee?"

Not on your life, I thought. *Every drop of coffee I sip for a little warmth now will still be with me six hours hence—and might even freeze intravenously.*

Looking back on that frosty experience, what I eventually came to understand is that we're all in a different place, even when we're sitting right next to each other. Scripture tells us: "Like clay in the hands of a potter, to be molded according to his pleasure, so are men in the hands of their Creator, to be assigned by Him their function." Sir, 33, 13. "For truly the potter . . . molds for . . . service each several article . . . As to what shall be the use of each vessel . . . the worker in clay is the judge." Wis 15, 7.

We've all got different roles to play, different jobs to do. Sometimes we're the driver, or the navigator, and we may have to endure cold for reasons unknown to us. Sometimes babies need blankets and it's up to us to make them, though our work may be uncomfortably sweat-inducing in a confined automobile. Even when we're side by side, and even when we're headed to the same destination, we have different things to do along the way. That holds true for parents and children, just like everyone else. The key is to let each other do the work we've been given, to help and not hinder others in their appointed duties, knowing that none of us are in charge. We're all on assignment. And we may have to make allowances to accommodate the tasks of our fellow pilgrims. So pack an extra sweater, just in case.

"It's never too late to be what you might have been."

George Eliot

45

Learning to Sing Like Saint Caedmon

Children have a way of reaching into your heart to find love you didn't even know was there. I was working away in the kitchen, trying to cook dinner and get the dishes done at the same time, when my daughters came in looking for Daddy.

"What are you doing Daddy?" Liz, our older daughter asked.

"Dadda!" our younger proclaimed.

"Are those our plates you're washing?" Liz asked. "Can I help?"

Liz reached for her stool so she could move it to the sink to help me. And whenever Liz is on her stool, her sister wants to climb up, too.

I was feeling too busy for help from two little people just then.

"I've got to get these dishes done," I told them, "and peel these potatoes to get them boiling." I grabbed a potato and held it up to show them, and was on the cusp of saying something like '*so I don't have time right now*,' when suddenly the sight of stool and 'tater combined to trigger a flash of memory transporting me back to when I was a kid and used to walk into my Mom's kitchen while she was working. No matter how busy Mom was, she never told me she didn't have time. She would stop what she was doing to talk to me. If she had to keep working, she'd cut me a slice of raw potato and sprinkle salt on it and tell me to grab a seat on the stool that was in her kitchen and then she'd talk to me while she worked.

I stood momentarily frozen, transfixed by a long lost memory. Where that little fragment of my past had been hiding amid the jumbled closets of my brain I have no idea. I hadn't thought about it in years and I didn't even know I had such a memory. But in an instant, I was right back in Mom's kitchen, seeing it all from the vantage point of that little stool while savoring the satisfying crunch of a potato slice.

I saved myself some future regret by silencing the words that had been about to form on my lips and instead said: "Hey, I've got a special treat for you two that you haven't had before. It was something I used to love when I was a kid."

I cut them potato slices, sprinkled a little salt on top, and they sat on their stool eating their new treat, looking happy and enjoying a chat with Dad. Our younger daughter's feet were swinging back and forth, still not able to reach the floor. When I looked down at her she held her potato slice out to me with bright eyes and exclaimed: "Dadda!"

"Yes, Honey," I answered, "tasty!"

I turned back to the dishes, and looking at the windowsill above the sink another piece of my childhood came back. My Mom had such a windowsill, and I remember a small brown vase she kept there. Times when I needed a little more than a potato slice, Mom would dry her hands on a kitchen towel, turn off the stove and say:

"Why don't we fill our little brown vase?"

She'd take me out and sit in the yard with me, combing through grass and clover hunting for violets. Then Mom would tie together all the flowers we had found with a blade of grass and put our diminutive bouquet in the tiny brown vase. It always made me happy to see it, and violets are still my favorite flower.

It was another bit of long-ago that I didn't know I was still carrying around. It reminded me of Mother Francis Raphael, O.S.D.'s description of St. Caedmon's transformation in her book *Catholic Legends*. Mother Francis Raphael related how Caedmon, a shy and "dull rustic hind," was awakened one night by an angelic visitor as he slept in the barn with the animals he cared for. The visitor told him: "Sing to me of the beginning of created things." Caedmon abjured, saying that he couldn't sing, and besides he didn't have any schooling, he was just a laborer, he couldn't compose a song. "Nevertheless," the visitor told him, "sing to me of the beginning of all created things." And so Caedmon tried. And when he did, much to his own astonishment, he found within himself a well of experiences to draw upon in singing of the glory of God's creation. As Mother Francis Raphael described it:

187

Then Caedmon felt a marvelous change in his soul: thoughts and shapes came flocking on his mind, and they were not so much new things as old things with a new light shining on them and making them glorious. The images traced in his memory through the long years he had spent in the broad forests and healthy uplands of his native land, seemed to start up fresh and beautiful within him. He heard the larks caroling sweetly in the morning air, as they were wont to do when he went early into the plough-field; and the mystic glory of many a sunset swam in golden floods before his eye, which he had been used to watch as he plodded home from his daily labour, scarcely knowing how much of their beauty was sinking into his soul.

Looking at the surprises I found within my memory, I had to wonder what made the images of those moments "sink into my soul" like the beauty of Caedmon's sunsets, to be dug out again by my own kids decades later. And I realized that it wasn't so much the potatoes or violets, beautiful as those things can be. It was the love behind those actions, those choices, that made those moments shine.

Scripture tells us: "Were one to offer all he owns to purchase love, he would be roundly mocked." Song 8, 7.

You can't buy love. Not for yourself, not for your kids. You can only choose love by choosing *to* love. That's what love is in the end: a choice. I can choose to keep my focus on myself and my own concerns—even when it's something as boring as chores—or instead to give myself and my attention to my kids.

And silly as it sounds, especially when the item of self-concern is something as boring and mundane as chores (which I really don't care that much about anyway), it's still actually really hard to break free from the gravitational pull of my own ego. Because it's not really about the chores, it's really about *my plans*. And that's hard to break free from. Particularly in the world we live in today, which is constantly sending the opposition message, encouraging us to keep our focus fixed firmly on ourselves. There are enticements to self-regard large and small, but whether those enticements come in the form of career, free-time, prestige, romance, vacations, new cars, or whatever (and the temptation can mutate into a thousand different shapes) the ultimate invitation is the same: choose the self over the other.

And as parents, we're uniquely situated to have that choice thrust upon us with some urgency many times each day. Kids have needs, demands, wants, and often theirs will conflict with our own, and so we have to decide—with exhausting frequency—whether we'll put our cares and interests and desires first, or demure and make way for those of our children.

As Bruce Marshall put it in *Father Malachy's Miracle*, it is the Christian challenge of "serving others and not self . . . a commandment so difficult that even the saints of God boggled over it."

For those of us who are parents, the others we are called to serve are first and foremost our children. And it is tough. But if it was enough to boggle the minds of saints, I guess it shouldn't surprise us parents if we find ourselves a little boggled from time to time, too. It's worth the difficulties, though. It's a tough calling, but it's also a grand calling—in fact, it's the calling of saints. And it was God Himself who gave us this task, so He must know there is more in us than we ourselves suspect. As St. Augustine wrote: "Do not you believe that there is in man a deep so profound as to be hidden even to him in whom it is?" If you've ever walked into a room and seen the little faces of your kids light up, and heard their giggles and exclamations of "Daddy!" as they jump up to run to you, and bent down to scoop them up in your arms . . . well, if you've felt that, you know St. Augustine was right. There's a greater depth of love within us than we imagine. It's there just waiting for us, if we, like Saint Caedmon, are willing to try.

"The glory of God is a man fully alive."

St. Irenaeus of Lyon

46

Thanksgiving

I was talking to my Dad on my cell phone one Sunday evening while I stood in the backyard flipping burgers on the grill.

"How was your weekend?" Dad asked.

"Fine," I said. "We didn't do much; the lake yesterday in the morning then cooked out some steaks in the evening. Today it was church in the morning, then the park, and now I'm grilling again."

My tone of voice conveyed my assessment of the weekend winding down: pretty pedestrian. Not a "Wow!" weekend, just *another* weekend.

A few days later I was at a wedding reception held in a grand old home from the turn of the century, now turned into a bed-and-breakfast, and painted along the top of the walls in the sitting room were lines from an Emily Dickinson poem:

Eden is the old-fashioned House
We dwell in everyday
Without suspecting our abode
Until we drive away

When I read those lines, it suddenly struck me how true it was in my life: how many blessings I have been given, and how I take them so much for granted. My wife and I and our children are all in good health, we live in a comfortable house that's dry in the rain, warm in the winter, and secure in the dark of night. We have plenty of food (and good food at that). We have our extended families and friends. We live in a country that's safe and free, where we can pursue the life we choose without threat or coercion. We are free to practice our religion (which means a lot more than the "freedom of worship" that is sometimes peddled as a sanitized and regulation-ready alternative). We are free to speak the truth without being thrown in jail. We don't fear being gunned down or having our homes burned because we are Christian. When we are expecting the blessing of a new baby we don't fear that armed government agents will break down our door to drag us away and kill the child in her mother's womb and then forcibly sterilize us. Nor do we fear that the government will seize our pre-school aged toddlers to begin indoctrinating them into military service. We don't fear starvation, pestilence, or disease. And all of these things are real fears and imminent threats to people just like me in many places all over the world, right now, every day.

Once my suburban American parish had a priest from Nigeria assigned to us as our associate pastor. The story of how he came to America is interesting.

His brother had also been a priest, and was martyred for the Faith in Nigeria. Our priests' bishop in Nigeria requested volunteers from among his priests for a missionary assignment. It was assumed among the priests that this was a request for men to go into that region of their country where Christians were being massacred and where our associate pastor's brother had already been killed. Knowing this full well, our associate pastor volunteered.

Surprise! Instead he was sent to a sleepy little parish in the suburbs of the American Midwest. That's how he came to be our associate pastor.

He was in our parish about three years, when he responded to another request for missionaries. Again, it was expected that he was being sent into danger in Nigeria. I shook hands with him after his last mass, and couldn't help but be stunned that this man was knowingly going where in all probability he would be killed. And he was doing it voluntarily. And with a smile! He actually seemed eager to go. It was a tremendous witness in the midst of our largely secularized culture grown comfortable and, as Father Barron termed it, "complacent in its finitude."

As it turned out, our associate pastor was in for another surprise. Like St. Anthony of Padua, our priest's missionary fields seemed elusive. This time he was sent to become a U.S. Army chaplain! He probably filled the role perfectly: he was made of the type of mettle needed to effectively minister to soldiers in uniform.

God puts His people where He needs them, even if it isn't where they expected to go.

I've taken our former associate pastor's surprising series of assignments as proof that courage and a willingness to follow God can lead us to adventures we never expected.

I've often wondered what our Nigerian priest thought of his time in our parish. I doubt he viewed the Faith, or the freedom to practice it, as casually as we sometimes do.

Thanksgiving is an American holiday. When I was in Holland once with an exchange group, I met a Dutch engineer who, upon encountering us bunch of Americans, told us about his one and only Thanksgiving. It was twenty years before, with some expat Americans working with him on a large scale engineering project in the Middle East. The Americans put together a make-do Thanksgiving, with an improvised dinner of chili and pizza (apparently turkey and pumpkin pie were scarce in the Middle East), and invited the Dutchman to join them. All those years later, the Dutchman still vividly remembered his singular Thanksgiving experience. Even though he never got to taste a genuine American turkey with all the trimmings, he associated Americans with this unique holiday. Maybe Thanksgiving is so distinctively an American holiday because we Americans have so much to be thankful for.

Of course freedom isn't free. That weekend I had told my Dad about while grilling in the back yard, which had seemed so pedestrian to me but which in actuality was so blessed, was the result of struggle and sacrifice by many people who fought, generation after generation, in places foreign and domestic, to win and preserve the freedom which they handed on to me, the freedom which makes possible the life I now enjoy. That freedom was given to me as a gift by others who earned it (sometimes at great cost to themselves), and entrusted it to us in this generation to safeguard during our brief time. And as Ronald Reagan said: "Freedom is a fragile thing." It's never achieved once and for all. It requires constant care and tending, preservation and defending. Reagan explained:

> Freedom is never more than one generation away
> from extinction. We didn't pass it to our children in

the bloodstream. It must be fought for, protected, and handed on for them to do the same, or one day we will spend our sunset years telling our children and our children's children what it was once like in the United States where men were free.

As Wayne LaPierre expressed it: "Freedom is never an achieved state; like electricity, we've got to keep generating it or the lights go out."

Having children really brings that point home. It's like Gandalf told Bilbo Baggins at the end of *The Hobbit*. In *The Hobbit*, Bilbo and his companions succeeded against all odds in a long and perilous quest, surviving many dangers by a hairbreadth to at last triumph over the forces of evil and win the great treasure they had set out to seek. Once the victory was secured, Gandalf told Bilbo: "You don't really suppose, do you, that all your adventures and escapes were managed by mere luck, just for your sole benefit?"

As a parent, I got my answer to Gandalf's question when I was putting one of our daughters to sleep at night. She was about one year old, and I was rocking her in the chair. She snuggled into me, looked up and said, "Happy, happy," with a big smile on her face and a twinkle in her eyes. Then she put her head on my chest and fell asleep, still smiling.

No, the blessings of America were not created just for my personal comfort and ease. Nor are they to be used or bargained away by me at my own private pleasure for my own personal considerations. The blessings of America are put into our hands for a time, but we hold them in trust for others. We can't know all the designs of God, or all the ways God will use us to touch the lives of others, or what all the ramifications will be from our faithfully discharging the responsibilities He has given us. Those ramifications will probably extend far beyond anything we can imagine. But whatever their ultimate reach may be, we know where it all starts. As Mother Teresa said: "Love begins by taking care of the closest ones—the ones at home." Our own children, those little ones entrusted to our care for so short a time, are among those intended beneficiaries of the blessings passed on to us by those who have gone before us.

The story of America is an amazing one—a miraculous one, the story of an angel in a whirlwind. Let's hope and pray—and work, and fight, and sacrifice—to keep that story—our story—alive for another generation. That's the responsibility entrusted to us. As also is the responsibility of preparing our children to do the same thing in their time, after we're gone, to preserve the gift of freedom for those who will come after them. On this unique American holiday, let us thank our Creator for the blessings given to us and our great nation, and pray for our angel in the whirlwind, the guardian angel of America, and give thanks for all those helping our angel in the battle to preserve this nation under God, with life and liberty for all, and ask God for the strength and courage we need to do our part in preserving those blessings in the days ahead.

"The only thing necessary for the triumph of evil is for good men to do nothing."

Edmund Burke

47.

First Week of Advent

Worthy of Prophecy

This is a true story. When we were kids there was a time when my sister Ruthie was the only girl in the family (besides my Mom). Ruthie had four brothers, and no sisters.

Well, Mom discovered she was pregnant again. Then Ruthie came down the stairs one morning and announced: "I'm going to have a sister on my birthday."

This was way before ultrasounds, back in the days when the only answer to the question: "Is it a boy or a girl?" was "Yes."

Ruthie really wanted a sister. But poor Mom was facing a tall order. Not only did Ruthie want a sister, she even wanted the sister born on her own birthday.

Mom told her: "We'll be happy with a boy or a girl, whenever they come, won't we?"

"Jesus told me," Ruthie answered. "In my dream He told me I'd have a sister on my birthday."

It turned out that Ruthie's dream was right.

On Ruthie's birthday our sister Agnes was born.

My wife and I also had a prophecy experience with our daughter. I started a new job, and a lady at my new work was known for her birth predictions. She successfully foretold two births in our office the year before I started. And this was nothing new for her. She'd always known when people were going to have babies prior to them becoming pregnant, and she could always tell whether the baby would be a boy or a girl.

When I started the new job, I shared an office with her. After about a month, before she'd met my wife, she had a dream that someone connected with the office was going to have a baby, and the baby would be a girl. But in her dream, she couldn't see the face of the woman who would become pregnant. Her

195

prediction quickened pulses all around the office. There was no doubting the potency of her prophetic proclivities. Pregnancy was surely imminent for someone, but who?

It turned out to be us. The pregnant woman's face was obscured in the dream because my office mate hadn't yet met my wife, but the prediction was spot on. Two weeks after the dream, my wife and I found out we were having a baby. We didn't have an ultrasound to learn the baby's gender prior to birth, but when the big day came and our child was born, she was a girl.

I know these experiences aren't unique. Everyone's got a baby prediction story. It's the very ubiquity of these premonitions that got me thinking: what is it about the birth of a child that stirs up prophetic powers?

Why not the stock market?

Instead of dreaming: '*You will conceive and bear a daughter,*' why not: '*Buy IBM at $15 and hold it for six months, then sell at $28.*'

Is there anyway to harness these prophetic impulses? I keep telling my sister Ruthie: "Before you go to sleep at night, think '*lottery.*'"

To no avail. Stocks and lotto's just don't get the prophetic juices flowing the way babies do.

As we head into Advent, and contemplate the role that the birth of a child plays in our salvation history, I think I can see why. It's the miracle of birth. As the mother told her sons in the second book of Maccabees: "I do not know how you came into existence in my womb; it was not I who gave you the breath of life, nor was it I who set in order the elements of which each of you is composed." 2 Macc 7, 22. Rather, "it is the Creator of the universe who shapes each man's beginning, as he brings about the origin of everything . . ." 2 Macc 7, 23.

The hand of God at work creating a new, eternal life. Now that's worthy of prophecy. Those are the kind of forces that will stir the prophetic impulse.

The chance to be part of God's creation of a new human life is a special thing. It's probably one of the few miracles in our lives where we will feel the reality of the eternal so tangibly, where we will have such a consciousness of God's workings.

In the hospital where our daughter was born, there's a "Baby Bell." It's a button on the maternity floor new Moms press after their babies are born, as Mom and baby are wheeled from the birthing room to Mom's recovery room. When a new mother presses the button, the Baby Bell chimes throughout the whole hospital.

The nurses explained that research has shown the ringing of a Baby Bell makes everyone in the hospital feel better. In hospitals there are people going through many things, encountering some of life's toughest moments, maybe encountering life's last moments. When they hear the Baby Bell, they know a new child is born, new life has come into the world, and they feel better. Just like the Star of Bethlehem announcing a very special birth brought joy to all mankind.

Jesus came into the world so that we "might have life and have it more abundantly." Jn 10, 10. This Advent, let's prepare for the miracle of that life.

"Our hearts grow tender with childhood memories and love of kindred, and we are better throughout the year for having, in spirit, become a child again at Christmas-time."

Laura Ingalls Wilder

48.

A Word About St. Nick's Day

St. Nicholas Day celebrates St. Nicholas, a 4th century bishop from Asia Minor who made secret nighttime deliveries of food and money to the doorsteps of the poor. The humble generosity of his secret aid-packages inspired others, and soon fellow townspeople were performing their own missions of clandestine charity. Today, St. Nick's memory is honored by the tradition of children placing shoes out in front of their fireplace before they go to bed at night on the eve of St. Nick's Day. St. Nick comes in the night to leave surprises for the children in their shoes, so when the kids wake up in the morning on St. Nick's Day (December 6), they find their shoes filled with small presents and treats.

Filling Soles on St. Nick's Day

Growing up, Saint Nicholas Day meant three things: the fireplace, stocking caps, and the biggest pair of shoes you could find.

It started the evening before, when we finished the family rosary. We always ended our rosary with the '*blowing of the candle.*' Well, actually it wasn't a candle, it was a little oil lamp that sat in the middle of the coffee table in our living room. Every night when it was time to pray we turned the lights off and Dad lit the lamp. Then, once the rosary was finished, we'd take turns trying to blow out the lamp from wherever we happened to be sitting. One of my brothers, Mighty Michael of The North Winds Lungs, could blow it out from the piano stool behind Mom's chair—a good 12 feet away—a truly prodigious feat of flame extinguishment. His was always *The Great Whiff Heard Round the*

198

Room. If he misdirected his stream of air and hit you instead of the lamp, your hair would ruffle in the breeze.

For St. Nick's Eve, the dousing of the light at the end of the rosary marked the beginning of anticipation. It was time to hunt up the biggest pair of shoes we could dig out from under the bed and place them in front of the fireplace. Our "Ranger Boots" were favorites for St. Nick's. These were leather hiking boots with long, lace-up ankles—the high tops of the forest, the kind of rugged bog and boulder bounders real wilderness rangers wore—with just the extra capacity that savvy St. Nick's veterans counted on for a bounteous early morning, hearthside harvest.

Loafers need not apply. Deck shoes, clogs, even my beloved gray suede BJ Pro's that I used for a whole season of cross country, none of them had any business in front of the fireplace on St. Nick's Eve. It was no time for fashion. It was time for performance, as measured by the haul the shoes could yield on the morrow. Cavern-osity was the criteria. Sheer, raw hollowness. You wanted shoes that could hold a ham. Shoes like Mark wore. The eldest, and a boy, Mark walked around on some monstrously massive romper-stompers, and he had the Sasquatch dimensioned dog-covers to go with them.

We lined the shoes up according to age in front of the fireplace. Shoes from the oldest child were at one end, the youngest at the other. That also meant they went from biggest to smallest. Mark's row-boats would be at one end, and Rachel's cute little mini-munchkin moccasins at the other. That row of shoes was a sight to see. You couldn't actually believe a real person wore some of them, either because they seemed so ridiculously huge or so unbelievably small. With the heels all even, the toes formed a sweeping curve cascading downward in size.

Next morning, the shoes were another sight to see: this time because they were stuffed to overflowing with St. Nick's largess, and right on top of the holiday heap would be the annual hat and gloves combination. We each got a new stocking cap and a new pair of gloves or mittens every year at St. Nick's Day, and I loved the hats. Many years Mom made them herself, and those were always the best. Even now, many a decade later, I still have a bunch of Mom's home-made noggin' warmers from St. Nick's Day, including a stocking cap with "Frost," our family name, knit into the bottom inside edge, so that it would show right-side up when you wore the hat and folded the edge up. I also have a gray hat with red snowflakes that Mom actually made for Mark to wear on his skiing adventures, but which I managed to commandeer somehow amid all the movings-in and movings-out over the years. The hats Mom made are thick, warm, and full of love. Mom told me once: "I always think about the person I'm making the thing for while I work, and I pray for them the whole time, so every stitch, knit, or hook is full of love and prayers. I hope you can feel that when you snuggle up in it." My sister Ruthie and her kids call Grandma's hand-made blankets "Forever Hugs," and they are perfect for a cold winter evening, curled up in a chair in front of the fire, with a good picture book and a little person in each arm.

Along with the hats and gloves, there was another surprise we knew would be hidden in our shoes every St. Nick's morning: candy cane pens. Shaped like candy canes with peppermint scented ink, they were an annual favorite—and they actually wrote really well. And they'd last all year. Those candy cane pens had to be the highest quality piece of holiday kitsch ever manufactured.

Another annual requirement was the ornaments. Every year, a new Christmas ornament would be in our shoes on St. Nick's Day, and Dad would write the year on the ornament. That's the kind of forethought only a father has. It's parents who really live with an eye toward the future. To look at those ornaments now, to touch them and re-live the memories they bring back, is wonderful—and also potentially frustrating if you couldn't place those memories in the context of your life. But thanks to Dad you can turn the ornament over in your hands and see the date on the bottom and say, "Ah yes, 1978, the year of the blizzard, I remember I was just 11 years old and . . ." It's amazing the power those tactile connections with our past have, their ability to put us right back in that place and time, with all its sights and sounds and smells.

Then there were the nifty little shoe sized gifts that changed every year but were always a delight. Things like miniature drawing pads and pencils. One year I got a pen with a radio in it. It was a real pen that really wrote, and it had a digital radio built into the handle, plus it came with headphones. I still have that one too.

There was just something about all those clever little items Mom found to fit in a shoe that appealed to the imagination.

And of course there were the chocolate gold coins, harkening back to St. Nicholas' gifts to the poor. The saint worked in secrecy, under the cover of night, leaving anonymous packages of food and money for those in need. And his secret missions of charity not only helped, they also inspired. As I've heard the story, St. Nick was the Bishop of Smyrna in present day Turkey, and when he saw people in need, he took it upon himself to give them his own food and money. But it was the way he did it that added the touch of romance which still captivates hearts and inspires wonder today, over a thousand years later. Because old Saint Nick snuck around at night like a mitered ninja, leaving his gifts anonymously. No one knew who was doing the good deeds. His secret, saintly style caught on, and soon other townspeople were doing the same thing, leaving their own clandestine gifts for their neighbors in need.

St. Nick's secret-agent-inspiration was the extra something special that, as Scripture says the Lord does for us, "buoys up the spirit, and brings a sparkle to the eyes." Sir 34, 17. It makes me think of Mother Teresa's advice to "do small things with great love." It's the kind of extra investment of the self that can transform mere blankets into Forever Hugs, stitched through and through with love and prayers. Which is what made those St. Nick's Days so special—the love and care and imagination that Mom and Dad invested of themselves to fill the soles, and hearts, of eight little souls entrusted into their keeping. The real joy of the holidays is that gift of self. I still have the hats and ornaments and radio pens from those St. Nick's Days, but I think the memories, and the warmth, and the sparkle in the eyes from those snowy mornings, will last even longer.

"If you hitch your wagon to a star, be sure it's the Star of Bethlehem."

Anonymous

49.

Second Week of Advent

Advent With King David

My wife and I sat on the couch, the room dark except for a glowing strand of colored lights wound around the Christmas tree and the flickering of candles in the Advent wreath. We'd just finished reading our Advent reflection and saying the Rosary. Now we sat together and watched snow swirl outside the window.

This time alone for the two of us was the cap of a wonderful winter day of adventures spent together as a family. We started with a leisurely morning, the whole crew gathered in Mom and Dad's bed, snuggling under blankets and "calculating" books (as our one year old calls 'reading') and watching snow out our window. When at last we roused ourselves to face the cold on the other side of the quilts, we made our collective way to the kitchen where we talked and cooked and finally sat down to a monster breakfast of bacon and eggs, coffee and juice, and a collection of 'outboard' dishes: toast and jam, fried potatoes, Poptarts and other assorted breakfast accoutrements.

Once we could move again, we bundled-up in hats and gloves and headed outside to enjoy the new snow coming down thick and fast. We ambled our booted way through the neighborhood, *Ooh*-ing and *Ahh*-ing at the Christmas lights and decorations on the houses, before stopping at the park for all things snow: snow-angels, snowmen, and of course snowballs.

We made it back home with all mittens and hats still intact and accounted for. Which called for a celebration of hot chocolate and snacks while playing board games. Every year we get a new game for the winter. This year it was *Boggle*, which has proven to be more congenial and to generate less competitive friction than *Scrabble* did last year. That's a good thing.

And so went our quiet, happy afternoon, the waft and warp of our day unfolding in a steady rhythm. The winter sun sets early in the upper Midwest, and it was already dark after dinner when we put the babies to sleep, singing Christmas carols for their lullabies.

With the little ones tucked in (at least for the time being), my wife and I sat on the couch, talking and working together as we sewed the "Christmas Puppy"—a stuffed animal for our older daughter for Christmas, made with all Christmas-print fabrics. I stitched an ear while my wife did the heavy lifting, sewing the body and filling it with stuffing.

While we plied needle and thread, we talked about our Christmas traditions, the things we'd already done and the things still to come, like the concert of Christmas music put on by the local college, and an annual production of Handel's Messiah, which is Daddy's favorite. We still needed to find a new Christmas story. We like to read stories out-loud during the vacation days around Christmas and New Year's, and we already have a healthy stable of annual regulars like the Nativity Story from Luke's Gospel, *The Best Christmas Pageant Ever*, *The Gift of the Magi*, and *A Cup of Christmas Tea*, but we always liked to work in at least one new book each year, searching for that still-to-be-discovered classic to add to our regular rotation.

Another tradition yet to be fulfilled: we still had presents to make. The gift exchange for our extended family has the twist that everyone is supposed to make their presents. In a pinch, you can buy something if you have to, but despite how crazy-busy life has become for everyone (there is a great gaggle of nieces and nephews spread all throughout the family), most people still manage to actually make something with their own two hands. The creativity is always surprising. Thinking about that got us talking about home-made presents from Christmases past. There was the pie-safe one of my brothers made for my Mom, with tin-stamped designs. The tool chest another brother made, and the shirt one of my sisters sewed for me which I still have and save for special occasions like Christmas Day and Easter.

As we reminisced, I was struck with how blessed we are. Here we were, warm, fed and free, secure with our loved ones. Very rare things in this world. Only a small fraction of the Earth's

6 billion people have so much. I couldn't help but wonder, why us? Why were we among the lucky ones?

It made me think of King David. David started life as a lowly shepherd. Then he became a war hero. Only to later be a wanted man, hunted by King Saul. But in time, David became king himself. The surprises kept coming. David, the shepherd boy and outlaw turned King, received an oracle in which God told David that God Himself would raise up a son from David's offspring who would be King forever, and God said: "I shall be a father to him, and he shall be a son to me . . ." 1 Chr 17, 13 -14. When David heard this, he went and "sat in the Lord's presence, saying: 'Who am I, O Lord God, and what is my family, that you should have brought me as far as I have come? And yet, even this you now consider too little, O God!'" 1 Chr 17, 16-18.

It's part of the wonder of Advent. With all that God has given us, there is something more and unimaginably greater yet to come. It's good to count our blessings and thank God for them, and to remember that we're called to be good stewards of all that God has entrusted to us, as the parable of the talents illustrates. And Jesus also said that whatever we do for the least among us we do for Him. But more important than the material gifts God gives us, even more important than the intangibles like our abilities and energy and time, is the gift of God Himself.

That is what Advent is about. God become man. God come to dwell among us. Come to redeem us. Come seeking His lost sheep—whether they live in a Newport mansion or a grass hut on the other side of the world. That is the gift that really matters: Jesus Christ. And it's been given to all of us, rich or poor, no matter the language we speak or the stars we see in the sky at night.

Still there is the question: Why? Why me? Why all of us? Why any of us?

Scripture gives us an answer, an answer that is simple, yet infinitely baffling in its mystery: Love. God loves "all things that are" and loathes nothing He has made. Wis 11, 24. Because "God so loved the world," Jn 3, 16, He chooses to give us the gift of His son, of Himself. Because He loves us.

50.

Third Week of Advent

Christmas Traditions

Scripture says "the preparation of a festive banquet is no light matter for one who thus seeks to give enjoyment to others." 2 Macc 2, 27. Parents working to make a special Christmas for their kids know how true this is.

When I was a kid, Christmas was my favorite time of year. So many little things added-up to a season of wonder. One day we'd come home from school to find Christmas garlands lining the banisters with green ivy and red bows, the Christmas village in the bay window, and the Christmas throw-rug my Mom hand-knit in front of the fireplace. We knew Christmas was on the way.

I remember Dad reading stories out loud, *The Best Christmas Pageant Ever*, *The Gift of the Magi*, and the Nativity story from the Bible, while we kids lay on the Christmas rug, with logs crackling in the fireplace and the smell of the Christmas tree filling the house.

We always had a real tree, and with all the wee ones in the house, Dad wired it in place so little hands wouldn't pull it down. The tree would be in a corner with wires stretched from tree to walls, where Dad screwed the wires right into the walls. Sometimes it ended up looking like an evergreen suspension bridge, but it always held.

Each of us kids had our own special ornaments for the tree. Every St. Nicholas day, tucked away amidst the chocolates filling the biggest pair of shoes we could find to leave out in front of the fireplace, would be a new Christmas ornament. Mom and Dad labeled them with the year. Now it's amazing to see numbers like "1970" on the ornaments and realize how far back these traditions go.

The Creche was a family treasure. The stable was hand-made by one grandfather, the Nativity figures came from the other. The manger started Advent empty. There was a basket of straw next to the stable and when we did something good, we were allowed to put some straw in the manger. We had to try our hardest to make a comfortable bed for Jesus in time for Christmas morning.

While we kids vied for rights to put straw in the manger, Mom baked like she was provisioning an army: cookies, fudge, caramel corn . . . bin after bin of deliciousness. Then there was the Advent wreath and lighting its candles every night during the Rosary, the Advent calendar . . . midnight Mass . . . so many memories, so many traditions.

Now that I'm a parent, I'm starting to realize that those memories and traditions didn't just happen on their own. Someone had to make them happen. And that meant lots of work. At Christmas, we kids were sponges soaking up Christmas cheer, while Mom and Dad were sponges getting squeezed to make it: creating joy takes effort.

I want to make memories like that for my kids, to leave them traditions they can pass on to their children one day. I just didn't know it would be so hard! But when the demands of the season seem overwhelming, it's good to remember what Jesus told us: ". . . the Son of Man did not come to be served but to serve and to give his life . . ." Mt 20, 28. "If I . . . have washed your feet, you ought to wash one another's feet . . . as I have done for you, you should also do." Jn 13, 14-15.

Parenting is a vocation of service. Even unto quite literally washing the feet of another. That's another memory we can leave our kids—and I don't mean the memory of washing their little baby feet. I mean the memory of parents working, with good cheer, to make a special holiday—an example of giving, serving, striving for another's joy. The sort of example that helps put Christ in the center of Christmas, not just through words (which are important too), but also through deeds. They may not appreciate the lesson now, but when it comes time for them to squeeze Christmas cheer out of their own souls, hopefully they'll have soaked up enough to be able to fill the next generation.

51.

The Season of the Unexpected

I was putting our younger daughter to sleep, and as we snuggled in the chair, I started singing: "Chestnuts roasting on an open fire . . ." She picked up the tune and sang the next line: ". . . Jack Frost *sniffing* at your nose . . ."

Christmas is full of surprises. Especially when kids are involved. Like with my brother and the buffalo cookies. One year when we were kids, one of my brothers used the annual cookie decorating party for more than a great adventure in licking frosting and consuming cookies (if a cookie breaks, you have to eat it, you know—can't have broken cookies on the silver tray come Christmas Eve). Instead of just filling up on sugar and Christmas tunes, my brother got creative and turned all the Christmas Tree cut-out cookies into buffalos. And they actually looked pretty good when he was done. Turns out that if you lay a Christmas Tree cookie sideways, cover the thick bottom part of the tree in dark brown frosting for a shaggy mane, frost the rest in a light tan, then add little frosting eyes and horns, you end up with a pretty convincing buffalo. At Christmas Eve there were no broken cookies on the silver tray, but there was a whole herd of bison.

Then there was Grisly Claus. We were making ornaments one year and another brother set out to construct a Santa Claus from red felt, googly-eyes, and cotton balls. Now, he was young, two or three at the time, and to his credit he did manage to put together some of the essential features of a traditional Santa Claus—hat, beard, and eye (only one)—but the effect of all the pieces together was something gestalt: the whole was more than the sum of its parts. And the whole was scary. With one wild googly-eye and a scraggly, lopsided beard of mangled cotton balls, and scars of glue and glitter across his cheeks and forehead, this

Santa Claus looked like he spent more time wrestling alligators—
or chainsaws—than filling stockings with candy canes. Us kids
loved it, of course, and immediately dubbed the ornament "Grisly
Claus" (or, as I prefer to think of it: "Grizzly Claws"—*rahr!*). It
was given a prominent place of display on the Christmas Tree, an
honor it still enjoys every year to this day. And you better watch
out, you better not cry, you better not pout, I'm telling you why: if
you do, Grisly Claus might just chew your arm off. So be good, for
goodness sake.

One of the very best surprises growing up was the Blizzard
of '78. I don't have the meteorological records in front of me, but
as I remember it, swirling snow blotted out the sun for days on end
and school was cancelled for weeks—right around Christmas and
New Year's, making for the longest Christmas break ever recorded
in the annals of formal education (and this was back in the days
before you had to make up snow days; life was good).

Our whole neighborhood was totally snowed in. Mom and
Dad pulled us around on our sled right through the middle of the
snow bound streets, meandering from street to snowy street, until
the sun set and we'd watch the snow falling in the yellow light of
the street lamps as we made our way home. J. R. R. Tolkien was
right, "Not all who wander are lost." Some have just found a
Winter Wonder Land, and they are enjoying it.

After a few days, Dad and some other men from the
neighborhood mounted an expedition to the grocery store. Dad
wrapped a scarf over his face and slung a burlap bag over his
shoulder. Mr. Farmer from across the street went decked out in full
Yukon trail breaking regalia: snowshoes, parka, waders, long red
scarf and a crazy hat with a fluffy ball dangling from its drooping
peak. Before setting out the intrepid Klondike Crew checked with
the old folks in the neighborhood to see what provisions they
needed to carry them through the storm (we had lived next door to
Mrs. Green for years, but never knew until then that she smoked
cigarettes). Once all the orders were in, the men folk ventured forth
into the driving wind. It was all very adventurous and pioneer, like
an episode from Little House on the Prairie, complete with the
surprise gift from the snow encrusted Santa-proxy when Dad
finally made it back to our door and produced a package of Boston
Baked Beans candies for us kids. Just like Mr. Edwards delivering

the Christmas parcel for the Ingalls' children: "It's too much Edwards, it's too much."

When there was finally a break in the snow, the men of the neighborhood sallied forth again, this time with shovels in hand. I suppose they probably made snow blowers even back in those days, but if they did, no one in our neck of the woods had one. The snow blowers around our parts were the husbands, huffing and puffing as they put their backs into the work.

The big dig on our street actually started with our Dad. He decided to blaze a trail through the drifts for our car to get out onto a plowed road. So, when the snow finally stopped, out he went into the chilly bright stillness of an early winter morning to clear a path to civilization. He trudged right into the middle of the street, and started shoveling. It must have been a surprising sight when neighbors wiped the frost from their windowpanes in the morning and peeked out, coffee cup in hand and sleep still in their eyes, to see one crazy man trying to shovel out a whole street by himself.

They decided to give him a hand. First one, then another, and before you knew it all the Dads on the block were out shoveling. The Moms started bringing out coffee and cookies to share around with everyone, the kids came running out to join in the excitement and play amid the snow flying from the shovels (and maybe even help a bit), and we ended up with a huge winter block party. People talked and shoveled and enjoyed good cheer, and in the end the whole street was cleared, and all the steps and sidewalks at the houses where the little old ladies' lived were shoveled, too.

And in the midst of this Season of the Unexpected we celebrate the coming of the King of Kings and Lord of Lords, the Lion of Judah—as a helpless little baby boy. Coming into the world with nothing, born in a stable, into a family poor and humble, at His birth He gave the world the greatest gift there ever was—Himself.

"For You are great and do wondrous deeds; and You alone are God." Ps 86, 10. An old piece of Christian wisdom is: when it comes to God, expect the unexpected. Prepare for surprise. Cultivate your capacity for wonder. For "He does great things beyond our knowing; wonders past our searching out." Jb 37, 5. Saint Augustine said: "If you understand, it is not God." C. S.

Lewis wrote in *The Lion the Witch and the Wardrobe*, "He's wild, you know. Not like a *tame* lion." And now is the time of the year to remember and celebrate one of God's deeds like no other: the birth of Jesus Christ. As Scripture tells us, "thank the Lord for such kindness, such wondrous deeds for mere mortals." Ps 107, 31.

Christmas Bells

I heard the bells on Christmas Day
Their old, familiar carols play,
And wild and sweet
The words repeat
Of peace on earth, good-will to men!

Henry Wadsworth Longfellow

52

Christmas

The Christmas Metamorphosis

I'm like a Christmas caterpillar. During the holidays, I put on a fuzzy sweater and eat my way through the season. By the Epiphany, the sweater is a little snug. But that's ok. I think of it as just a phase in my evolving yuletide metamorphosis, as I pass through different stages of development on my way to finally taking flight on beautiful Christmas wings.

Mostly, though, it seems that by the end of the Christmas season I just need a bigger sweater.

I haven't quite made it all the way to the Christmas wings yet. But now that I have kids, I think I may be getting closer.

The first stage in my Christmas evolution was when I was a kid myself, and Christmas meant "Wonder." The whole season was filled with expectancy and a special kind of wintery awe. With the coming of Christmas, everything changed. Our house became festooned with red and green from garlands and wreaths decorating our door and stairway and the dining room buffet. A Christmas tree filled the house with the scent of pine, and the colored lights twined among its branches glowed softly during evening prayers. Coffee tables and countertops sprouted all manner of Christmas oddments, from snowman shaped candy dishes to miniature books of Christmas classics like "The Night Before Christmas." Crèches, candles, and cookies were all part of the once yearly transformation of our humble abode into a magical land of Christmas wonder.

Our daily routine changed along with the domestic decor. Advent candles were added to our nighttime prayers, and we began opening the little doors on our Advent calendar. We even had a second Advent calendar that Mom made special for after school. It was a giant cloth wall-banner with little pouches sewed on it, one pouch for each day, and each was filled with treats. First thing when we got home from school we'd all run to the Advent banner and it was one person's turn each day to open the next pouch.

Another tradition was putting straw in the manger for Jesus whenever we did something good, so we could make a soft bed for Jesus by the time He was born on Christmas day. And for one month every year *The Fiddler on the Roof* was supplanted from its place of primacy in the regular rotation on Mom's record player to make way for the soulful stylings of Johnny Mathis and Nat King Cole singing the Christmas classics.

Even the world outside changed. I grew up in the Midwest around the Great Lakes, and winter meant cold and snow—lots of snow, "deep and crisp and even." Icicles sparkled, a million criss-crossing tree branches were traced in white, and night settled early over the land. Days were filled with sledding, ice-skating outdoors, and snow forts. Nights we'd lie on our backs in all the dark and quiet, staring at the sky, feeling the feathery, cold touch of snowflakes as they settled on our cheeks and eyelashes, until Mom finally made us come in. Robert Service described the winter wonderland perfectly in *The Spell of the Yukon*:

> The winter! the brightness that blinds you,
> The white land locked tight as a drum,
> The cold fear that follows and finds you,
> The silence that bludgeons you dumb.
> The snows that are older than history,
> The woods where the weird shadows slant;
> The stillness, the moonlight, the mystery
> I've bade 'em good-by – but I can't.

And though "the Great White Silence, not a snow-gemmed twig aquiver" (from *The Call of the Wild*, also by Robert Service) that Service wrote about was the Yukon territory of the Far North, our much tamer Midwest winters were still enough to bring us kids a feeling of amazement and smallness in the face of something mysterious and grand and greater than ourselves.

It all combined to fill Christmas with a sense of wonder.

The next phase of my Christmas development began somewhere around the high school years. The nature of Christmas started changing. The sense of wonder began to recede into the background. It wasn't that I consciously came to consider Christmas less wondrous than I had previously. But busyness, of all varieties and seemingly ever expanding and accelerating, began to fill our lives, displacing the quieter spaces and less scheduled moments that are the natural habitat for wonder to grow and flourish. There were sports and clubs, jobs and friends. Every morning we all hied off in a hundred different directions pursuing our varied and disparate endeavors. An unintended and unexpected consequence of this was that we began to spend less and less time with each other, and more with classmates and teammates and co-workers.

When we reached the point that the first of us graduated from high school, it became even more pronounced. Suddenly we didn't even live under the same roof anymore. From then on, each August meant a new departure from our little home, as someone else packed up to head off to college. For each expectant new freshman-to-be, Mom sewed the same going-away present: a "College Quilt" in the colors of their new school, to keep them warm and cozy in their dorm room loft. The night before the send-off, we'd all gather in the living room for cake and the unveiling of the new quilt. The next day we'd help pack the departing sibling's stuff in the trunk of our parent's car, then wave good-bye as Mom and Dad drove them off to some distant school. It was funny, the more quilts Mom made the emptier the beds got at home.

And once people started graduating from college and taking jobs, we all got to know what busy was really like. It's a shame you don't realize how much free-time you actually have in college until you've left it behind. Oh the hours I would love to reclaim! But there's no going back, only forward, and the pursuit of careers has a way of drawing people off to far distant cities. It all happens so fast that in the thick of it you don't realize the ramifications of what's going on. Only in retrospect do you discover that a page was turned somewhere back along the way, and things will never again be as they once were. I remember moving out of Mom and Dad's house to take my first job in another city. One morning of loading boxes into my brother's pick-up truck, an afternoon of driving, and then unloading on the other end in a place I'd never lived before, and that was it. By sunset I no longer lived at home, and never would again. At the time, I wasn't aware what a major life change was underway. I was mostly worried about finding a place for dinner that night and getting my telephone service hooked-up (those were in the days before cell phones). I never paused to think that I wouldn't be seeing Mom and Dad everyday anymore, or that my time with my other siblings would henceforth be dramatically curtailed.

But even if I wasn't conscious of the loss at the time, I still felt it. During those years, what I most remember about Christmas was the eagerness to see my family again. I wanted to re-connect with my brothers and sisters and Mom and Dad. And I wasn't alone in feeling the emptiness of that absence. In the weeks leading up to Christmas Mom became a clearing house for travel information, as all of us kids were constantly calling her for the latest updates: who was going to make it home and how long would they be there? Did John get the days off work? Had Rachel bought plane tickets yet? Was Mark getting a full two weeks?

Then, when at last the office Christmas parties were finally over, the travelling commenced. If you plotted all the individual journeys on a map, you'd see eight red lines, each originating from different starting-points sprinkled all across the country, all converging via plane, train and automobile on one little dot on the map: a forgotten little spot deep in the heart of the snowy Midwest, a spot that held no significance whatsoever to the great wide world, but which meant everything in the world to the people gathering there in a small, happy home. One-by-one the arrivals trickled in over several days until at last everyone was together again. And then—let the fun begin! Days we'd go ice-skating, out to lunch, or hack around on our musical instruments playing songs together. We also spent a lot of time laying on couches in front of a roaring fire, wrapped in all those quilts Mom had made over the years, snacking and snoozing and reading. Sometimes if you walked in it would make you chuckle. You'd see five or six people all together in one room, sprawled out on furniture, only their feet and heads showing from under the mounds of blankets, and everyone silently reading their own book. It was during these years that we developed the "Most Boring Book Contest." Whenever the spirit moved someone, they would call out: "Most Boring Book Contest!" and then each of us in turn would read the very next line of our book out loud. As a group we'd discuss the relative merits of each literary offering and award one person's tome the uninviting title of "The Most Boring Book." Mostly it was just funny to hear the lines from such wildly different books juxtaposed with one another. Snippets of Louis Lamoure westerns take on a whole new flavor when interwoven with Maeve Binchy romances and Tolkien hobbit tales. Jokes would fly as the contestants argued for the non-boringness of their own beloved book and cast aspersions on the selections of their rivals. When the designation of "Most Boring Book" was finally bestowed by general acclamation, the banter subsided back into a contented silence broken only by the soft sounds of turning pages and a crackling fire.

But the absolute highlight of Christmas in those years was the nights. We'd stay up all night talking. It was no wonder we spent so much of our days laying on couches, because we gabbed through the wee small hours every night, night after night. After dinner everyone gathered in the family room for games, usually Trivia Pursuit or one of its many offshoots. Questions and answers—or more often questions and guesses—would be interspersed with discussion, and gradually discussion would digress more and more until eventually the trivia cards were forgotten and we were just talking.

Those were good times. We were all just starting out in life, launching for the first time, whether it was beginning college or our first job, and everything was new and fresh. We were all adventuring into uncharted territory, and we shared with each other our experiences and impressions of the big wide world out there.

It's funny how things change.

Now all of us kids are married, and most of us have kids of our own. We still stay up all night, but now it's to tend fussy babies. The last time I was home for Christmas, I met one of my brothers at my parents' kitchen sink at 2 a.m. as we were both making bottles. When we had finished and were tiptoeing back upstairs on Mom and Dad's creaky, old, wood staircase with the nectar of somnolence in our hands (that's "formula" for you laymen), we met one of our sisters walking her daughter in the hallway. Under those circumstances, conversations tend to be short and hushed—as in monosyllabic and whispered.

It somehow seems appropriate, though, to have Christmas filled with caring for babies. After all, the arrival of a baby is what it's all about—"the reason for the season," as they say—and babies can show us much about Christmas. Like reminding us of possibilities. Holding a little baby in your arms, you can't help but wonder: who will this little person be? What will they do? Where will they go? What will they make of their life? The possibilities for that baby's life are real and palpable before your eyes as you cradle the baby in your arms. And then, you realize, it's not just this little baby: our life too has possibilities. There is still an open question as to what *we* will do, what we will make of our life, what we will be. No matter where we are in life's journey when the realization strikes, it remains true. The final destination is still open and up to our choosing. It may take a little more courage, a little more truth, more faith, hope, and love than we've put into living so far, but despite the difficulties, we know the possibility is there for us. Christmas is about those possibilities. God hasn't given up on us. God sees possibilities in us we can't even imagine for ourselves. That's why He came. "For God so loved the world that he gave His only Son, so that everyone who believes in Him might not perish but might have eternal life." Jn 3, 16. "For God did not send His Son into the world to condemn the world, but that the world might be saved through Him." Jn 3, 17. And so He came, as a little baby—a new life come into the world—that we might have life also, "and have it more abundantly." Jn 10, 10. Christmas is about, at least in part, remembering that life and the possibilities it opens for us. Christmas calls us to a metamorphosis that can still be ours. Christmas celebrates a miracle, a miracle of new life.

Made in the USA
Las Vegas, NV
14 November 2024

11803179R00125